Instructor's Manual with Tests
for

SOCIAL WELFARE

Instructor's Manual with Tests
for

Johnson • Schwartz • Tate

SOCIAL WELFARE
A Response to Human Need
Fourth Edition

Prepared by
Charles L. Schwartz

Allyn and Bacon
Boston • London • Toronto • Sydney • Tokyo • Singapore

Contents

Preface iii

Part I: Societal Welfare as a Response to Societal Concern 1

Chapter 1: An introduction to the social
welfare system 3

Chapter 2: Social change 13

Chapter 3: Poverty, human needs, and social welfare 19

Chapter 4: Social welfare resources 29

Chapter 5: Racism and discrimination 37

**Part II: Two Attributes of the Social Welfare System:
Social Work and Fields of Practice** 47

Chapter 6: The emergence of the social
work profession within social welfare 49

Chapter 7: Income maintenance as a response
to human need 61

Chapter 8: Child welfare services 71

Chapter 9: Health care and social welfare 83

Chapter 10: Social welfare and mental health 93

Chapter 11: Social work and corrections 103

Chapter 12: Gerontological social work 113

Chapter 13: Organizing fields of practice
by system type: groups, communities
and families: 121

Chapter 14: Old new fields of practice:
industrial and rural 133

Part III: The Contemporary Social Welfare System 141

Chapter 15: The contemporary social
welfare system 143

Preface

The Social Welfare System: A Response to Need is intended for use at the undergraduate level. The most appropriate use of this book is as a textbook for the first, or introductory, social work course. The text could be used as a primary or supplemental text in courses carrying the titles: Introduction to Social Work, Introduction to Social Welfare, or Introduction to Social Work and Social Welfare. These courses are usually designed to introduce students to the emergence of the social welfare system. The overall focus of this text is the examination of social welfare and social services delivery systems as responses to human need. Emphasis is also placed on developing understandings of the social work profession and its roles in the delivery of social welfare and social services.

An Outline of the Text

Part I. Chapters 1 through 5. Chapter 1 examines the historical milestones in the emergence of the social welfare system and the social welfare arrangements used by society to respond to human needs.

Chapters 2 through 5 examine social problems/conditions which have brought about human need. Chapter 2 discusses the phenomenon of social change and its relationship to social problems/conditions which cause human need. Chapter 3 focuses on the problem of poverty. Chapter 4 discusses the concept of resource distribution, and the impact it has had on the emergence of human needs to which society has responded through the provision of social welfare services. Chapter 5 deals with the social problem of racism and discrimination.

Part II. This part of the text focuses on two important attributes of the Social Welfare System—the profession of social work and fields of practice. Chapter 6 discusses the historical development of social work, with particular focus on the close ties between its development and the historical development of social welfare. It also examines the professional requirements for practice and discusses professional practice issues. Chapter 7 through 15 examine the fields of practice of social work and focus on specific problems or population groupings including: income maintenance, child welfare, health care, mental health, gerontological social work, groups, communities, families and industrial and rural social work.

Part III. Chapter 15 provides a framework by which to analyze the functioning of the contemporary social welfare system and discusses current issues in social welfare.

We have tried to make this book easy for beginning social work students, who are basically unfamiliar with the social welfare system and the profession. The primary purpose of this instructor's manual is to provide a link between the teacher and the textbook. The assumption is that instructors will supplement the content of this textbook with appropriate materials, illustrations from practice, and locally relevant content that will enrich their student's learning. Student learning patterns and styles and instructor teaching styles are diverse; therefore, no specific assumptions are made or preferences given as to how the content of this textbook should be taught. Teaching aids for some of the content of the chapters are provided for teachers who desire to use them. We hope that instructors will use the material creatively and in ways compatible to their own teaching style. We also realize by the time this text becomes available that some of the material, particularly policy material, may have changed or be in the process of change. We encourage instructors to be aware of such changes and to deal with them in ways deemed appropriate, given the current situations.

The manual presents possibilities for use by the instructor for each chapter under the following headings:

A. A summary of key points and issues developed in the chapter.

B. Major concepts or understandings students should internalize.

C. Teaching aids or exercises the instructor can use to assist students in learning the materials presented in the chapter.

D. Questions that can be used for study or class discussion as essay examination questions.

E. Objective (multiple-choice) examination questions relative to the materials in the chapter.

Instructor's Manual with Tests
for

SOCIAL WELFARE

Part I

Societal welfare as a response to societal concern

The chapters in this section introduce students to the basic concepts of social work and provide a framework for understanding the social welfare system and the arrangements used by that system to provide for the needs of people. They also contain material that will assist students in developing an understanding of the historical development of social welfare.

Much of the material presented in Chapter 1 is historical. It is important that students recognize the relevance of this history as they develop understandings of the social welfare system. Students may be "turned off,, to these historical materials at first, but the instructor can assist students by supplementing and integrating current developments and issues and illustrating their relationship to the historical material. In chapters 2 through 5, students examine the conditions that make it difficult for individuals and families to meet their own needs. Social change, poverty, resource availability and racism and discrimination are discussed as well.

These five chapters provide an introduction to materials that will be presented more specifically in Part 11. It is important that students gain an overall understanding of the social welfare system before acquiring specific understandings about its respective parts.

Chapter 1

An introduction to the social welfare system

Chapter 1 introduces the student to the concept of social welfare and the historical development of the social welfare system. It introduces concepts that are discussed in more depth in subsequent chapters of the text. The goals are: (1) to assist the student in developing a beginning frame of reference by which to view how the social welfare system responds to human needs through various social welfare arrangements; and (2) to help the student identify the motivators and underlying influences that have shaped the development of the systems and the responses it has made over time.

A. Key points and issues

1. Human needs refers to resources that people need to survive and function appropriately in the social situation of which they are a part. Each individual and family has needs. When these needs are met, families are able to function more adequately. Some human needs are common to all people (e.g., sufficient food, clothing, and shelter); yet, needs do vary, depending on the individual or family and their social situation. Specification of the needs of people must consider their life style, culture and value systems.

2. It is important to consider how human needs are met. The value of "rugged individualism," the belief that people should be responsible for meeting their own needs, has influenced the processes by which this occurs. The issue is raised that this value is neither possible nor, in fact, desirable in contemporary society relative to optimal human growth and development. People have always depended on others to help them secure the resources to meet their needs and, at the same time, providing for the common good. There must be a balance between meeting the needs of individuals and families and meeting the needs of society to maintain the common welfare.

3. The formalized means by which society responds to human needs is the social welfare system. Social welfare is the system

3

of arrangements, programs and mechanisms designed to meet human needs, particularly those needs individuals and families cannot meet with their own resources. The social welfare system refers to both informal and formal mechanisms, governmental and non-governmental arrangements. It is important to emphasize that students consider all societal efforts to respond to human need, not just governmental mechanisms.

4. Six societal arrangements that are used as responses to human need are identified. They are: mutual aid, charity-philanthropy, public welfare, social insurance, social service, and universal provision. Each of the arrangements has qualities that make it particularly useful for meeting needs under certain circumstances. The advantages and disadvantages of each are discussed. Discussion of these arrangements provides a beginning framework by which students can begin to evaluate the social welfare system's response to human needs from an historical and contemporary perspective.

5. The authors use an historical approach to discuss the development of the social welfare system by noting milestones along the path of its development. The milestones discussed are of two types: specific legislation and institution/agency development. To add to the understanding of the milestones in the development of the system, the influences involved are presented. The influences are of two types: situational and philosophic. Situational influences include economic, social and political events. Philosophic influences are values, beliefs and prevailing philosophic constructs. The milestones discussed are: 1) English Poor Law 1601; 2) the development of Institutional Care 1820-1850; 3) the emergence of COS and Settlement Houses 1885-1900; and 4) the Social Security Act of 1935.

6. The authors provide an analytical framework through which the students can develop an understanding of how decisions are made about informal or formal arrangements used in meeting human needs and what factors influence those decisions. Macorov developed the framework in his book *The Design of Social Welfare*. In it, he discusses motivators for social welfare programs. They are: mutual aid, religion, politics, economics, and ideology. These motivators are discussed as to how they have influenced the development of the contemporary social welfare system.

7. Ideological differences in perceptions of welfare and different responses to human need exist in various regions of the United States. They are influenced by local or regional customs, ethos, and cultures that can be traced back historically to the original inhabitants of the region (e.g., British, German, Italian, Scandinavian, etc.) Regional ideological differences are also due to the presence of minority groups (Native Americans, African-Americans, and Hispanic-Americans). The groups have culturally specific patterns for providing for the needs of individuals and families. Their mere presence has led to the development of prejudicial attitudes and discriminatory practices that have greatly influenced the local implementation of governmental social welfare programs.

B. Teaching this material may be somewhat difficult, as the chapter presents an overall view of social welfare and a general discussion of the historical development of the social welfare system. Later in the text, much of the material will be presented in more detail, specifically as it applies to the development of social work as a profession and the development of social welfare and social services delivery systems. Therefore, it is more important in the early chapters to emphasize general views rather than specific details. Students must begin to formulate understandings of the concepts at this point in order to understand materials presented throughout the remainder of the text.

Students should develop the following:

1. An understanding of and an ability to define human needs.

2. Knowledge about areas of human need and the factors that influence specification of need.

3. An understanding of how human needs are met through both informal and formal means. Students should also be developing an awareness of their own values relative to the issue of individual versus societal responsibility for the meeting of human needs.

4. An understanding of the six societal arrangements used to respond to human needs and how they have impacted the development of the social welfare system from an historical and contemporary perspective.

5. An ability to cite examples of each arrangement for meeting human need used in the United States social welfare system.

6. An appreciation for the significance of the historical milestones in the overall development of the social welfare system and the situational and philosophic influences that contributed to the milestones.

7. A knowledge of the five motivators for social welfare and how each has influenced the development and structure of the U.S. social welfare system.

C. It may be difficult to engage students in the learning of this material because the material is largely historical and most students have had limited direct experience with the social welfare system. The authors recommend that learning activities focus on assisting students to understand the relevance of the past as it has influenced the development of the contemporary system.

Suggested learning activities

1. To assist the students in understanding the relationship between human needs and the social welfare response, divide the class into groups and have them review the list of human needs identified in this chapter. Then have them discuss the following:

a. the issue of individual versus societal responsibility for meeting human needs;

b. who is primarily responsible—the individual, society or both;

c. which needs should be the primary responsibility of the individual;

d. which needs should be the primary responsibility of society and what can society provide via social welfare arrangements, formal, informal and governmental, in response to meeting these needs;

e. when, if ever, does the individual's responsibility for meeting their own needs end.

2. For the purpose of assisting the students in developing general understandings of the six arrangements for social welfare service delivery, divide the class into groups and assign each group one or more of the arrangements. Have them discuss in their group and make an oral report to the total class on the following:

a. the definition and nature of the arrangement;

b. the historical development of the arrangement;

c. the impact of the historical development of the arrangement on the contemporary social welfare system. Does its influence continue in today's system;

d. the benefits, services, or programs provided to people in each arrangement;

e. the advantages and disadvantages of each arrangement;

f. the changes or alternatives to the arrangement they would suggest.

3. Provide a piece of case material to each group and request that the students prepare a report on how they would respond to the needs of people and the problem/conditions specified in the case using the arrangement(s) assigned. Emphasize that they be realistic in their report as to the constraints and limitations associated with each of the arrangements.

4. For the purpose of assisting students in understanding that regional-local differences in people's perceptions of ,'welfare,, may be based on regional or local values, ethos, customs, attitudes and cultures, and that their own perceptions of ,'welfare,, were likely influenced by the local or regional environment in which they were socialized, engage the students in the following learning activity.

Divide the students into small groups. Designate one student as the group's recorder.

1. Each student in the group identifies his/her own home locale and region of the state or country.

2. Each student briefly discusses their own perceptions of "welfare.,,

3. Each student discusses whether they believe their own perceptions are either similar or different than those of their parents or significant others in their environment.

The designated recorder for each of the groups records the following:

1. each student's home locale and region of the state or country;

2. each student's perceptions of "welfare,,;

3. the similarities between each student's perceptions and the perceptions of significant others in their environment.

Activity B

Each group analyzes their recordings and determines the following:

1. patterns of similarity in perceptions of students from the same region of the state or country;

2. patterns of difference in perceptions of students from different regions of the state or country.

The instructor may also want to collect the recordings of each group and engage the entire class in a discussion of the patterns of difference in student perception of "welfare,' specific to particular regions of the state or country.

The instructor would also have the opportunity to introduce other variables that might explain differences (e.g., religion, urban-rural geographical locations, national heritage).

D. Class discussion and study questions

1. What are human needs? How do they vary from individual to individual, family to family? What factors must be taken into consideration when determining the needs of individuals or families?

2. Discuss the issue of individual versus societal responsibility for meeting human needs. In what instances or circumstances should individuals be responsible for meeting their own needs? In what instances or circumstances does society have an obligation to meet the needs of people?

3. What is social welfare? What are its purposes? Should social welfare be conceptualized as encompassing a broad range of programs to assist people or be limited to programs which assist people with certain needs?

4. What are the component parts of the social welfare system as discussed in the text? What is meant by informal and non-governmental mechanisms or arrangements?

5. Which of the six arrangements for social welfare services delivery are designed more to assist people who struggle with meeting their own needs? Which are available to benefit the social functioning of all people?

6. What are the differences between the arrangements of mutual aid and charity philanthropy? What are their advantages and disadvantages?

7. What are the differences between the arrangements of public welfare, social insurance, social service and universal provision? Discuss the advantages and disadvantages.

8. Which of the arrangements do you believe should be the primary social welfare response for the future?

9. Discuss the historical milestones in the development of the social welfare system. What situational or philosophic influences were involved in these milestones? Of what relevance are these historical milestones to the development of the contemporary system?

10. How have the social welfare motivators — mutual aid, religion, politics, economics, and ideology—influenced the development of the social welfare system?

11. What factors explain ideological differences in perceptions of welfare in different parts of the United States? How are local and regional responses to human needs influences by these differences?

12. How does the presence of minority groups in certain regions of the country influence the implementation of governmental social welfare responses.

E. Objective (multiple choice) examination questions

1. The concept *human needs* refers to:

   a. financial resources people need to survive.

   X b. resources people need to survive and function appropriately in their social situation.

   c. resources some people need to maximize their individual growth and development.

   d. resources people need to solve problems.

2. When considering individual versus societal responsibility for meeting human needs, the position taken by the authors is:

   a. individuals are always responsible for meeting their own needs.

   b. society is responsible for meeting the needs of all people.

   X c. Given the situation or circumstance, both the individual and society are responsible for meeting human needs.

   d. individuals should first attempt to meet their own needs and if they fail, society becomes responsible.

3. The concept *social welfare is:*

   a. a system of arrangements, programs and services that has developed over time.

   b. has a purpose to meet human needs.

   c. is made available to particularly assist individuals and families who cannot meet their needs with their own resources.

   X d. all of the above.

4. Informal arrangements or mechanisms for meeting human needs are:
   a. services, benefits, or assistance provided by governmental structures.
   X b. assistance provided by family, friends, neighbors, and other natural helping systems.
   c. assistance provided by both natural helping systems and governmental structures.
   d. assistance provided by churches and other religiously-based organizations.
5. The arrangement of mutual aid as defined in the text is:
   a. the provision of support (e.g., food, clothing, shelter, health care) to persons unable to support themselves by governmental social welfare structures.
   X b. the helping activities of people who assume responsibility for assisting one another outside of formal community structures.
   c. intangible benefits or services provided by agencies or institutions which provide assistance in the area of social functioning.
   d. the provision of economic assistance or other services by governmental units, which are available to benefit the social functioning of all persons.
6. The major disadvantage of the arrangement *universal provision* as discussed in this chapter is:
   a. some people would continue to "fall through the cracks,, in the system.
   b. this arrangement runs counter to the American value of "rugged individualism,, where people are expected to support themselves.
   X c. cost. Universal provision of social welfare programs is more costly than other arrangements of service delivery.
   d. no stigma is placed on receiving of benefits.
7. The arrangement of social insurance is:
   a. another term describing assistance provided to people unable to meet their own needs funded through general tax revenues.
   X b. funded through contributions made by insured workers and employers, where the recipient is paid the benefit under an insurance arrangement.
   c. funded by local and state tax revenues.
   d. a program of assistance provided by private philanthropic agencies.

8. Which of the following is *not* a major provision of the English Poor Law?

    a. local control. The poor are the responsibility of the local government unit.

    b. residency or settlement

    c. families are responsible for the care of their own relatives in need.

X d. all people deserve assistance. Non-categorical assistance was provided.

    e. certain categories of people are more deserving of assistance than others.

9. The Social Security Act of 1935:

    a. forms the basis of the contemporary social welfare system.

    b. provides benefits under a social insurance arrangement.

    c. provides benefits and services under a social welfare arrangement.

X d. all of the above.

10. Which of the following ideologies as motivators for social welfare have influences against the universal provision arrangement in the belief that this would be a disincentive to individuals providing for their own needs?

    a. altruism and humanitarianism

X b. free enterprise and rugged individualism

    c. politics and economics

    d. mutual aid and religion.

11. Ideological differences in perceptions of welfare and responses made to human need in different parts of the United States are most influenced by:

    a. liberal or conservative attitudes of the people living in different parts of the country.

    b. economic and political conditions existing in different parts of the country.

X c. customs, ethos, and culture of descendants of the inhabitants of different parts of the country.

    d. Religious beliefs of people in different parts of the country.

12. The presence of minority groups in particular regions of the United States affects the meeting of human needs in which of the following ways:

X a. the implementation of local governmental social welfare response to human need.

b. their presence has no effect on local governmental social welfare responses.

c. the local governmental social welfare response may favor minority group members over those from the majority group.

d. more funding is available for local government social welfare responses in areas where minority groups reside.

Chapter 2

Social change

Chapter 2 introduces students to the concept of societal change and how social change has affected U.S. society. The authors develop the theme that problems in meeting human needs and societal responses to human need via the social welfare system increase during times of accelerated social change. As well, they introduce students to the viewpoint that provision for human need and social control are related to and have influenced the development of the contemporary social welfare system. As the student gains an understanding of the balance between meeting human need, caused in part by social change, and maintaining social order and control, they will learn how the social welfare system in the United States society functions .

Social change is considered from five perspectives.

1. Societal Paradigms and ideologies that influence responses to social change and provisions for meeting human need.

2. Society as a social system: how change that occurs in societal social systems brings about change in the functioning of the societal system, which in turn impacts the meeting of human need .

3. Change brought about by industrialization, the growth of the monetary economy, population trends, political philosophy and scientific and medical advances impacts societies, ability to meet human needs via the social welfare response.

4. The impact of the above change on the social functioning of individuals and families in contemporary U.S. society.

5. Empowerment of individuals, families and other collectives of people whose lives are negatively affected by societal responses to social change and human need.

Understanding the nature of social change and its impact on society as a whole and the individuals and families who comprise it contributes to a framework through which students can analyze the goals or missions of various social welfare arrangements discussed in later chapters in the text.

13

A. Key points and issues

1. Problems in meeting human needs and societal responses to human needs increase during times of accelerated social change.

2. The contemporary social welfare system has as a mission: to provide for unmet human need to the extent and means by which this occurs.

3. U.S. society is a social system, and changes (e.g., economic, political, or social) will affect the functioning of the overall system, the functioning of individuals and families, and the provisions the system makes for meeting human needs through various social welfare arrangements.

4. Social change engendered by dominant societal paradigms, technological advancement in science, medicine, the growth of the industrial monetary economy, political philosophy and population trends have victimized some individuals and families, resulting in unmet human need.

B. This material is important for beginning social work students to learn as it helps them gain an understanding of how human need arises, a major theme presented throughout this text, and develop a framework through which to analyze the formation of social policy that creates the provision of social welfare services.

Students should develop the following.

1. Beginning understandings of a social systems approach as one means of explaining the existence of social problems.

2 Understanding the impact of population changes on the development of the U.S. social welfare system.

3. Understanding that the shift from a subsistence economy to a monetary economy has affected individual and family capacity to meet basic needs.

4. Ability to identify the changes that have taken place in family structure and how these changes impact the family's capacity to meet the basic needs of its members.

5. Understanding that some people become victims of social change, and the ability to identify examples of this in contemporary U.S. society.

C. Instructors can be creative in developing class learning activities to assist students in understanding this material.

Suggested learning activities

For the purpose of assisting students understand how social change brings about human need in society and the impact of that change on the social welfare response to that need, divide the class into groups and ask each group to pick a topic of social change from a list provided by the instructor (e.g., the AIDS problem, pro-life/pro-choice debate, teenage suicide, etc.). Then have the students discuss the topic using the following questions as a guide.

1. What human needs have been caused by the social change?

2. How can these needs be met while maintaining provisions for social control?

3. What responses should be made within the societal social system to deal effectively with social change?

4 What responses should be made via the social welfare system to respond to the needs of individuals or families affected by the change?

D. Classroom discussion or study questions

1. What societal changes, other than those discussed in this chapter, have brought about changes in government's responsibility for ensuring the welfare of its citizens?

2. What kinds of provisions for human needs resulting from social change should government provide? Which level of government should be responsible?

3. Should social welfare provision be used as a means of social control?

4. How can a social systems approach be used to explain the existence of social problems? Give examples.

5. How has social and technological change in the current century brought about changes in family structure, roles, and functions? In what ways has this caused instability in some families?

6. How do changing family structures and functioning affect the need for social welfare services? Give examples.

7. What impact have changes in population characteristics and economic systems during the previous and current centuries had on the functioning of society and how it responds to human need?

8. What groups of people in U.S. society have been affected most by social change? What specific needs have emerged in these groups? How has their social functioning been affected?

9. Is social change desirable or should it be avoided? What are the conservative and liberal progressive views relative to this question?

10. How are poverty, hunger, and homelessness in the United States related to social change?

11. How can empowerment be used as a strategy to assist people who are affected in negative ways by social change.

E. Objective (multiple-choice) examination questions.

Choose the *best* response.

1. A social welfare arrangement that developed as a result of the impact of social change in U.S. society is:

   a. institutional care

   b. charity organization societies and settlement houses.

   c. Social Security Act of 1935.

   Xd. all of the above.

2. The major goal of the provision of social welfare is:

   a. to provide for unmet human need.

   b. to maintain social order and control.

   X c. both of the above.

   d. to provide only for the needs of certain groups of people.

3. According to a social systems view, as social change takes place in society, mechanisms that have been developed to maintain society also will change. Change occurs in:

   a. economic structures.

   b. political structures.

   c. institutional structures.

   d. societal expectations of the roles and functioning of individuals and families.

   X e. all of the above.

4. Social change in any of the functional sub-systems of the societal social system will bring about a need for change in which of the following ways?

   a. development of new mechanisms for social control

   b. Development of new provisions for meeting human needs

   c. Some parts of the system continue to operate under old roles, others adapt to accommodate for the change

   d. Has an impact on the individual's and family's capacity for social functioning and meeting their own human needs

   X e. all of the above.

5. A societal change which has affected the response to human need via social welfare arrangements is:

   a. population shifts relative to size and rural to urban residence.

   b. age distribution.

   c. a dependence on a monetary economy.

   d. changes in family structure and functioning.

   X e. all of the above.

6. A population group whose social functioning has been particularly affected by societal social change is;

   a. the aged.

   b. the poor.

   c. families.

   X d. all of the above.

7. How has social change during the current century affected families the most?

   a. Caused changes in family structure.

   b. Caused changes in family roles and functions.

   X c. Contributed to a lessening in cohesiveness and stability in some families.

   d. Contributed to the disappearance of family mutual aid.

8. Changes in values about the importance of the family to the individual have contributed to:

   a. economic instability in some families.

   X b. the "we centered individual,, who places great value on the importance of the family to himself/herself.

   c. the lack of attachment of the individual to his/her family.

   d. a unified family social policy which places emphasis on strengthening the family as a unit.

9. A conservative political view relative to the desirability of social change holds that:

   X a. Social change should be avoided in favor of the maintenance of the status quo.

   b. social change is desirable and should be pushed for to create better conditions of living.

   c. social change should neither be avoided nor pushed for, but should occur naturally on its own.

   d. social change will occur, nothing can be done to avoid it.

10. A negative consequence of social change as it affects indi-

viduals within society is:

a. lack of capacity to meet their needs or those of their family.

b. lack of capacity or opportunities to learn new skills or knowledge enabling them to adapt to maintain their social functioning.

c. alienation of the individual from other persons and society, resulting in a loss of self-esteem and capacity to adapt and cope. X d. all of the above.

11. Dominant societal paradigms about the meeting of human needs are those that are:

a. supported by the majority and those who are socially and politically affluent.

b. Embedded in societal , institiutional and social structures.

e. responsible for shaping the thinking and responses made to human needs and problems.

X d. all of the above.

12. Empowerment in Social practice challenges social workers to:

a.engage in the helping process as a partnership with bothworker and client involved in mutual decision making and problem solving.

b. focus on client strengths and adaptive capacities, skills and competencies.

c. assist social structures and institiutions to respond more humanely to human need.

X d. all of the above.

Chapter 3

Poverty, human needs, and social welfare

This chapter is devoted to an extensive discussion of the social problem/condition poverty, with the aim of providing students with an understanding of the relationship between poverty and human needs and an understanding of the responses that have been made to deal with its effects through the social welfare system. Hopefully, the student will gain an awareness that poverty is a complex and destructive social problem/condition that is deeply rooted in the total structure of U.S. society and that its solutions are equally complex and elusive. The chapter focuses on definitions of poverty, discussion of who are the poor; how poverty is measure; the causes of poverty; the responses to poverty made via social welfare, both in the past and present; the responses of social work as a profession to poverty; and the problem of homelessness in the United States, a related social problem that has a cause and effect relationship with poverty.

A. Key points and issues

1. No single social problem/condition has been more troublesome nor has had such an effect on the U.S. population. Thirteen percent of the population had incomes below the poverty line in 1989.

2. Throughout history, numerous attempts have been made to eliminate or reduce the level of poverty in the United States. The social welfare system is the primary mechanism for facilitating these programs.

3. Poverty persists, despite the provision of social welfare and other anti-poverty programs and services.

4. Poverty is difficult to define. It can be defined by society at large, by societal institutional structures such as government, by individuals or groups who experience it, and/or through theoretical orientations (e.g., economic, sociological/cultural/racial, and political). Although economic definitions are the most practical and useful, it must be viewed through all these realms to be understood.

19

5. The Social Security Administration determines the official poverty line using the formula described in the text. It is adjusted each year for inflation; thus, it has risen steadily over the years. Several criticisms have been made about how the poverty line is calculated.

6. Certain groups of persons in U.S. society are affected significantly by poverty. They are: racial and ethnic minorities, the aged, women, children, the working poor, persons in rural areas of the United States, the homeless, and a group of persons, referred to as the underclass, for whom poverty is a permanent life reality.

7. Poverty has a number of causes which fall into three primary areas of cause: economic, social and political. These areas of cause are inherent in the societal social structure. Although poverty is mainly an economic problem and its primary cause is related to the functioning of the U.S. economy, the remaining areas of causation exacerbate its effects on the U.S. population.

8. Throughout history a number of responses to poverty have been made by the social welfare arrangements and other anti-poverty programs and services. The first responses were through private philanthropy and charity and were begun in the late 1800s and early 1900s. During the 1930s the social welfare programs created by the Social Security Act of 1935 formed a permanent response to poverty. In the 1960s Congress created as separate response to poverty through War on Poverty programs administered through the Office of Economic Opportunity. Since the 1970s national interest in poverty declined; however, recently renewed interest in poverty has emerged as a result of political and social events.

9. Historically, social work's responses to the poor in the late 1800s and early 1900s were responsible, in part, for the development of the profession. As the profession continued to develop, it began to move away from working exclusively with the poor. The public social welfare system, however, continues to be the largest employer of social workers. Professional organizations, such as NASW and APWA, whose membership consists largely of social workers who have remained quite active in advocating for the poor. Arguments continue to exist as to the appropriate role of the profession relative to poverty.

B. This material should be considered an essential part of an introductory social welfare course. The authors believe that exposing students to this material contributes to socialization into the profession. It is likely that upon entrance into the profession, and throughout their careers, students will work with the poor in every field of practice. Therefore, students need to become sensitive to and gain understandings of poverty and the poor so they will be prepared to intervene with those in poverty and deal effectively with social policy issues that affect the poverty population.

Student should develop the following.

1. The ability to define poverty from several points of view.

2. Understanding of the way the federal poverty line is determined.

3. Understanding of the three sociological theories of poverty and the strengths and limitations of each in explaining the existence of poverty.

4. Understanding how the view points, culture of poverty and social inferiority have influenced societal perceptions of the poor.

5. Understanding of the various causes of homelessness and its various forms.

6. Capacity to discuss the economic causes of poverty.

7. Ability to identify specific groups within society that are particularly in danger of being in a poverty situation.

8. Understanding how political views affect concerns for poverty as a social problem.

9. Ability to identify social and situational factors that affect societal perceptions of poverty.

10. Ability to identify and trace the history of societal responses made to poverty.

11. Ability to identify philosophical stances and responses made to poverty by the profession of social work.

C. Because of their social status, most students may be somewhat naive about poverty issues. Exposure to this material may be a real "eye opener,' for them as they gain an understanding of and sensitivity to the problem. The instructor may also encounter students who are struggling with their own values relative to poverty. It is important that class learning activities focus on students gaining an overall understanding of poverty. More importantly, there should be a focus on developing sensitivities to the problems of the poor and on developing positive perceptions of the poor.

Learning activities and exercises

1. To assist students in understanding the effects of poverty on persons from vulnerable groups in society, and to develop an awareness of their own value perceptions about them, divide the class into groups, provide them the following situation, and ask them to deal with the questions that follow the case situation.

   Case situation: A woman with three school-age dependent children has been deserted by her husband. He has taken all the financial resources, but she has household goods and a place to live. She is unemployed and has no financial resources. The husband was the sole provider. Although she may be able to find a job, her skills are such that it would be a low-earnings job.

   Questions:

   1. What is your immediate "gut level" reaction or feeling about this woman's situation? Do you think there is a relationship between your reaction and the values you hold about people who are poor?

   2. What are the potential effects of poverty on this family? How might this woman and her children be significantly affected by poverty?

   3. What difficulties will this woman likely encounter in the employment market? Are any of these difficulties related to her lack of job skills? What other factors might restrict her abilities relative to gaining employment?

   4. If a poverty lifestyle continues for this family, what potential effects would it have on the children?

2. To assist students in understanding that the development of social policy and programming to deal with the problem of poverty are complex and difficult, divide the class into groups and have them work with the following situation.

   The federal government wishes to develop long-term solutions to the poverty problem. They have appointed you to a national task force to develop social policy that would create a new permanent anti-poverty program. A research group, formed prior to the appointment of your task force, has completed a study and is submitting the following recommendations or alternatives to you for consideration.

   1. The establishment of a flexible poverty index which would enable persons and families to be eligible for anti-poverty programs on at least a partial basis.

2. The creation of a program of employment (jobs), both part- and full-time, that would pay above minimum wage, with residual benefits of health care, child care and job training.

3. The creation of an income maintenance program that is universal and developmental in nature rather than categorical and more generous benefits than existing programs.

4. A system of social services designed to assist persons to overcome the problems associated with a poverty lifestyle. Employment and job counseling should also be included.

In your discussion of these recommendations and alternatives, consider the following issues and questions:

1. What are the positive and negative aspects associated with each of the recommendations?

2. What values do you think are reflected in the recommendations provided?

3. What are the social, political, and economic ramifications of each of the recommendations?

4. What recommendation(s) would your group select as being the most appropriate and viable solution to the problem of poverty?

5. How would you proceed to implement the solution?

D. Class discussion and study questions

1. Why is poverty such a complex and destructive social problem? Why has no single social problem/condition been more troublesome in its effects on the U.S. population.

2. Why is poverty difficult to define? Why are economic definitions of poverty more practical and useful? Why is it also important to define poverty in social/cultural and political terms?

3. Four sociological theories of poverty were discussed in the text. What are the strengths and limitations of each relative to promoting understandings of poverty?

4. How is the poverty line in the United States determined and by whom? How is the poverty line used in distinguishing the poor from the non-poor?

5. What groups in the United States are particularly and significantly affected by poverty? Which groups experience a more situational type poverty? Which group experiences poverty as a permanent life reality?

6. What factors have studies identified recently as being causative to the problem of homelessness? What responses are being made to this problem?

7. Discuss the view that the primary economic cause of poverty is an unequal distribution of income throughout the population. Which mechanisms are employed to redistribute income? Why have they failed to do so in such a way as to eliminate poverty?

8. Discuss the conservative, the radical-conservative, and the liberal views associated with the causes of unemployment. Which view seems to be valid in explaining why unemployment exits?

9. Discuss the view that the poor are politically disadvantaged. Why has poverty become more of a political issue in recent years? Is this interest likely to continue?

10. Which responses to poverty were made in the late 1800s and early 1900s through private philanthropy and charity? Were they successful?

11. Although New Deal programs provided temporary relief to ease the plight of the Depression, why did it become necessary that the United States deliver a more long-term response to poverty, resulting in the Social Security Act of 1935?

12. Which events brought about an awareness of and sensitivity to the poverty problem during the early 1960s? Which anti-poverty programs were created by the Economic Opportunity Act of 1964?

13. Which factors contributed to the lack of success of the anti-poverty programs of the 1960s? What were some of the positive contributions of the anti-poverty programs of the 1960s? Have their innovations lasted to the present time?

14. What are the arguments presented relative to social work's lack of interest in poverty issues?

15. Is there a need for the profession of social work to begin to assume a more aggressive leadership role in the development of national social policies dealing with poverty?

E. Objective (multiple choice) examination questions. Choose the *best* response.

1. Poverty can be defined:

   a. by society at large.

   b. by the individuals who experience it.

   c. in economic, social/cultural, and political terms.

X d. all of the above

2. The poverty line in the United States is calculated by:
   a. comparing all incomes and determining an average income as the poverty line.
   b. distinguishing the poor from the non-poor.
   X c. determining the amount equal to 3 times the amount of the economy food plan established in 1955.
   d. comparing regional differences in the cost of living as listed by the Consumer Price Index.

3. According to the culture of poverty theory offered by Oscar Lewis:
   a. poverty forms the basis for a separate and distinct culture.
   b. the poor have developed norms, values, attitudes and lifestyles which differ from the rest of society.
   X c. both of the above.
   d. persons from racial groups have low motivation and genetic deficiencies that prevent them from achieving economic status.

4. Which of the following groups of persons are particularly and significantly affected by poverty:
   a. racial and ethnic minorities.
   b. aged.
   c. women.
   d. children.
   e. working poor.
   X f. all of the above.

5. A group of people for whom poverty is a permanent reality is:
   a. the homeless.
   X b. the underclass.
   c. the unemployed.
   d. low-income families.

6. Which of the following is the chief economic factor that causes poverty?
   a. unemployment/underemployment
   X b. unequal distribution of income throughout the population
   c. inflation
   d. inadequate income supports

7. The view of unemployment that holds that poor persons do not have access to jobs or thenecessary education or skills to secure them is:
   a. the conservative view.
   b. the radical-conservative view.
   X c. the liberal view
   d. the Restrictive Access view.

8. Which of the following social factors contributes to the incidence and perpetuation of poverty?

   a. blaming the victim

   b. American values of self-reliance and self-sufficiency

   c. seeing the consequences of poverty but ignoring the causes

X d. all of the above

9. Crisis poverty, a typology developed by Alan Little, holds that:

X a. poverty is caused by a catastrophic event which renders the person unable to meet their own needs.

   b. poverty is a natural consequence caused by the demands of living.

   c. poverty is a reaction to the unwillingness of the person to be self-sufficient.

   d. poverty life styles are inherited.

10. Political leaders may be insensitive to the poor mainly because:

   a. the poor don't vote.

X b. the poor do not contribute to campaigns of political officials, so there is no incentive to represent their interests.

   c. the philosophy that the poor are poor because they want to be.

   d. the poor are not sufficiently organized as a special interest group.

11. Poverty, as demonstrated during the Depression years, is:

   a. a problem of the individual

X b. an economic problem with the potential of affecting large numbers of people.

   c. a problem of isolated groups.

   d. a problem of racial minority groups.

12. The anti-poverty programs of the 1960s were authorized by Congress by the passage of:

   a. War on Poverty Act of 1960.

   b. Opportunity Assistance Act of 1962.

X c. Economic Opportunity Act of 1964.

   d. Anti-poverty Act of 1963.

13. Which of the following factors contributed most to reducing the success of the anti-poverty programs of the 1960s?

   a. poor administration

   b. lack of funding

X c. priorities in funding — more funding was given to the Vietnam War than the war on poverty

   d. graft and corruption.

14. Renewed interest in poverty as a social problem in recent years has:
    a. caused considerable debate in Congress.
  X b. put poverty back on the national social policy agenda.
    c. resulted in new anti-poverty legislation.
    d. brought about the emergence of a collective voice for the poor in determining social policy on poverty.
15. Evidence that suggests that social work is not doing enough relative to the poverty situation is:

    a. other groups (e.g., the middle class), have captured more of the profession's attention and resources .
    b. harmful language used by social workers when referring to the poor.
  X c. both of the above.
    d. none of the above

Chapter 4

Social welfare resources

Chapter 4 introduces students to the concept of resources, those things individuals and families must have to live and function effectively in contemporary U.S. society. The materials presented develop the notion that people have a variety of needs that must be fulfilled if they are to live satisfying lives, and that there are a variety of resource systems available to people to meet their needs Resource systems considered include: (1) personal resources: self, family and friends; (2) informal resources: natural helping systems in communities and self-help groups; (3) institutional resources: schools, churches and social welfare organizations, agencies and institutions. The authors also address conditions and attitudes that influence resource distribution, issues of accessibility and acceptability of resources, and how diverse groups within society gain access to and use of available resources. The material is presented to promote the students, understanding that the meeting of human needs is contingent on the availability of resources to meet those needs. Students tend to conceptualize resource in a formal, institutional framework (i.e., the social welfare system). The students, understanding of resource systems available to meet human need is broadened by discussions of these various resource systems.

A. Key points and issues

1. Human beings have a variety of needs that must be met if they are to live satisfying lives. These include food, clothing, shelter, health care and safety. As well, humans have a desire for emotional, intellectual, social-cultural and spiritual development.

2. These needs are met usually within the three major resource systems: personal, informal, or institutional .

3. Individuals need appropriate resources to carry out expected roles and tasks assigned by society and lead satisfying lives.

4. Services are those resources that are provided by and require the activities of professionals employed within the formal social welfare system

5. When adequate resources and services are not available to individuals and families, there is the potential for impaired social functioning. This leads to a need for expensive societal responses, such as income maintenance or institutional care.

6. The range of resources and services needed by a person or family for optimal functioning within society is vast, changes from time to time, and varies depending on the diverse characteristics of the person or family. Areas of needed resources addressed are economic, parenting, marital relationships, interpersonal and community relationships, physical and mental disabilities. Delivery systems discussed include: schools, hospitals and other formal institutions, community organizations, information and referral services, and counseling and therapeutic services.

7. Those resources that people need to achieve adequate social functioning can be identified relative to various stages in the life span.

8. Another way of understanding the need for resource provision is to identify resources usually provided to individuals and families in a personal social support network, the absence of which can lead to social dysfunctioning. When resources provided in personal support systems are absent, or when needs are beyond the capacity of the support system to provide, the social welfare system is called upon to provide resources that will fill the void.

9. Preventative resources and services provide a means to avoid a breakdown in social functioning and further dysfunction when breakdown has occurred. The authors discuss the types of prevention modes of preventative services, barriers to prevention and policy issues associated with prevention.

10. Availability of resources means that they are present in sufficient quantity so that all who need them have an opportunity to use them. Quantity in and of itself is not sufficient in determining availability. The means of distribution, accessibility, usability and coordination must also be considered.

11. U.S. society contains a diversity of cultures and life styles. Human needs and the resource systems needed to satisfy those needs should be seen as diverse and dependent on the culture and lifestyles of the person or family.

B. The instructor will need to utilize additional literative resources when teaching this material. It is important that beginning social work students be exposed to this material. It helps them conceptualize that human needs and the resource systems available to meet them must be considered from a holistic viewpoint, taking into consideration issues of social support networks, prevention, availability, accessibility, coordination, usability, and the effect of human diversity issues on resource provision. This introductory background will enable students to acquire further knowledge and skills in subsequent course work relative to resource availability and provision.

Students need to develop the following

1. An understanding that individuals and families have a variety of needs that must be met if they are to live functional and satisfying lives.

2. Ability to identify and describe the five mechanisms for meeting human needs.

3. An understanding of the three major resource systems available to meet human need: personal, informal and institutional, and the range of resources provided in each.

4. An understanding that when adequate resources and services are not available, individuals and families may experience impaired social functioning.

5. An understanding that resources and services needed by an individual or family change over time, are diverse, and are associated with stages in the life span.

6. An understanding that resources needed by individuals and families can and should be provided through social support networks.

7. An ability to define social support networks and to discuss its importance of supporting individual functioning.

8. An ability to define prevention and to identify the three types of prevention.

9. An understanding that availability of resources in contemporary society is contingent upon their quantity, distribution, accessibility, usability and coordination. The problems associated with all of the above sometimes prevent individuals or families from having their needs met.

10. An understanding that human needs and the resource systems needed to satisfy them should be conceptualized in a human diversity framework.

C. Instructors can use a variety of learning activities to assist students in mastery of this material. Instructors have a choice between using didactic learning activities or more experiential or "hands-on,, type learning activities utilizing case materials.

Suggested didactic learning activities

1. Have a speaker from a self-help group explain the purposes of the group and how it functions.

2. Have a social work practitioner from a community social welfare/social service agency discuss resource availability in the community, and how that worker uses community resources in their work with clients. What factors are considered in resource provision?

3. Have a speaker from an information and referral center (if available in your community) speak to the class on their work in assisting people in finding community resources.

Suggested experiential learning activities

1. Divide the class into small groups. Provide each group with a community resource directory. Ask each group to identify community resources that fall into the following categories: (1) informal (such as self-help groups); (2) institutional (such as church, school, or social welfare organizations and agencies). Have them support their choices with material from the text.

2. Divide the class into small groups. Provide each group with a piece of case material. Ask the students to identify the needs in the situation (e.g., basic living needs, health care, safety, emotion, intellectual, social-cultural or spiritual). Using the framework in the text for determining the range of resources that may be needed, ask them to identify the specific areas of resource or services that they feel would be appropriate for the case situation presented. Also have them consider the needs and resources from the life-span formulation, a social support network perspective and a preventative basis.

3. Using the same example have them attempt to identify factors discussed in the text that would affect the availability of resources given the diverse characteristics of the person(s) involved in the case example.

D. Class discussion or study questions

1. What human needs must be met if individuals or families are to live functional and satisfying lives?

2 Discuss the specific resources that fall within the three major resource systems—personal, informal and institutional.

3. What are resources? What are services? What do they enable the individual or family to do?

4. What range of resources and services do you think the social welfare system should provide to an individual or family?

5. What are personal social support networks? Which resources do they provide? What is likely to occur with individuals or families when resources usually provided by social support networks are absent?

6. What are prevention resources and services? What types of prevention exist? Should primary prevention be a priority of social policy? What barriers or policy issues affect the delivery or provision of preventative resources and services?

7. In determining the availability of resources, is the quantity of resources sufficient to determine their availability? What other factors need to be taken into consideration?

8. What problems in distribution of resources exist in the U.S.? What can be done to correct these problems?

9. What does the diverse nature of individuals or families have to do with their human needs and the resource systems available to meet them?

10. What problems are caused by the discontinuity between cultural life style considerations and the delivery of services.

E. Objective (multiple choice) examination questions. Choose the *best* response.

1. Which of the following areas of need must be met if an individual or family is to live a functional and satisfying life?

   a. basic living needs (e.g., food, clothing shelter)

   b. health care/safety needs

   c. emotional/intellectual growth needs

   d. social-cultural-spiritual needs.

   X e. all of the above

2. Natural helping systems and self-help groups would fall into which of the following categories of resource systems?

   a. personal resource system
X b. informal resource system
   c. institutional resource system
   d. life-span resource system

3. Resource and services needed by individuals and families are:

   a. vast
   b. change over time.
   c. vary depending on diverse characteristics.
X d. all of the above.

4. According to the text, resources are:

   a. activities of helping professionals employed by the social welfare system.
X b. what individuals and families need to survive and carry out the roles and tasks society expects of them.
   c. only available to those who can afford to pay for them.
   d. available only to certain categories of individuals and families.

5. Services can or should be provided by which of the following?

   a. governmental units
   b. personal networks (e.g., families, friends)
   c. community natural helpers
   d. community institutions
X e. all of the above

6. When resources usually provided to individuals and families by a personal, social support network are absent or when needs are beyond the capacity of the support system to provide, what usually occurs is:

X a. dysfunction in the individual or family.
   b. adaptation to the lack of resources are made by the family or individual, appropriate functioning continues.
   c. personal coping skills are used by the person or family and appropriate functioning continues.
   d. social support networks disintegrate.

7. Primary prevention resources are:

    a. those resources or services that deal with present difficulties to prevent their further occurrence .

X b. those resources or services that assist in prevention the occurrence of dysfunction in persons or families.

    c. those resources that provide treatment or rehabilitation to persons or families experiencing dysfunction.

    d. those resources or services designed to identify and assist "at risk" populations.

8. The availability of resources to support individuals and families in their social functioning is contingent on:

    a. a sufficient quantity of resources.

    b. distribution of resources.

    c. accessibility/usability of resources.

    d. coordination of resources.

X e. all of the above.

9. The distribution of the services and resources within the social welfare system is:

    a. adequate to meet the needs of most persons.

X b. inadequate and a problem within contemporary society.

    c. controlled by government units.

    d. controlled by private/voluntary sectors of the social welfare system.

10. Resources and services are more readily available in:

    a. large metropolitan areas.

    b. in areas where citizens have a high level of social consciousness.

    c. in areas of economic affluence.

X d. all of the above.

11. The usability of resources and services is affected by which of the following factors?

    a. language barriers

    b. cultural barriers

    c. attitudes and approaches of those who deliver them.

X d. all of the above.

12. The lack of coordination of services and resources may lead to:

    a. additional burden to already burdened people.

    b. duplication of services and resources.

    c. fragmentation of the service delivery network.

X d. all of the above

13. The contemporary social welfare system makes assumptions about the needs of individuals and families based on:

a. the culture of values of the people served.

b. how the needs are presented by the person at the time the service is provided.

X c. the culture, values and perceptions of need of the white middle class.

d. the services available within the system.

14. The resources and services made available to meet human need should be based on:

X a. the culture and life styles of the persons involved.

b. what can meet the needs of most persons.

c. meeting only the needs of the truly needy.

d. "the wheel that squeaks the loudest gets the most grease."

Chapter 5

Racism and discrimination

This chapter allows students to examine the social problems/ conditions of racism and discrimination and develop understandings about the cause and effect relationship between racism and discrimination and the meeting of human need within our society. Students will begin to gain an awareness of the complex and destructive nature of these problem/condition areas, as well as insight into their impact on the most disenfranchised members of our society. The authors, major theme is that racism and discrimination against diverse groups within U.S. society limits and restricts their participation within the mainstream of society and has denied access to resources, including social welfare. The experiences and reactions of minorities of color (Blacks, Native Americans, Hispanics, Asians) and other diverse groups (e.g., aging, women, developmentally disabled, ethnic groups and gays and lesbians) to racism and discrimination are discussed. Critical views are also expressed as to how the social welfare system and the profession of social work have responded to these groups. Hopefully, students will begin to examine the issues that confront the social welfare system, the profession and society in dealing with these problems.

Students should also develop an understanding of the human diversity perspective. This perspective provides a useful framework that will assist them in analyzing the functioning of diverse groups within our society, avoiding the stereotyping of members of these groups, and identifying what the social welfare systems and professional social workers can and should be doing about the problems/conditions of racism and discrimination, particularly the use of empowerment as a strategy to combat racism and other forms of oppression.

A. Key points and issues
1. Racism, prejudice and discrimination are social problems/conditions that have contributed to unmet human needs within U.S. society.

37

2. Racial and other diverse groups either have been denied access to the resources necessary to sustain an adequate quality of life, or resources and services have been delivered in a manner that makes them incongruent within their particular cultural frameworks, thus rendering them unusable.

3. Racism, prejudice and discrimination have been used interchangeably to describe the conflict between the majority society and minority racial, ethnic and diverse groups, but each has its own meaning.

4. There are two closely related forms of racism: individual racism and institutional racism.

5. Socioeconomic class must also be considered. Often socioeconomic class characteristics and racial characteristics become confused, causing the development of stereotypical attitudes toward all persons of color.

6. Each of the predominant minorities of color have a long-standing history of struggle in achieving equality within the mainstream of U.S. society. Each has engaged in a civil rights movement, consisting of both violent and non-violent efforts.

7. Among the many "isms" that describe discrimination against diverse groups are ageism and sexism. Discrimination against the aged and women are the most obvious forms of discrimination other than racial discrimination.

8. Other diverse groups in our society are victimized by discrimination. They are the developmentally disabled, the mentally ill, ethnic groups, religious groups, gays and lesbians.

9. Philosophically, the profession of social work has always been concerned about racism and discrimination. However, prior to the 1960s, the profession's responses to the problems were minimal. From the 1960s until the present time, a concerted effort has been made within the profession to address these problem/ condition areas. The majority of the response has been through professional organizations such as NASW and within education through the efforts of CSWE.

10. A recent development within the curriculum of the schools and within the profession at large, has been the adoption of the human diversity perspective, a framework for examining the functioning of diverse groups and organizing the knowledge and skills needed to intervene with diverse groups.

11. Although the profession has adopted the human diversity perspective, the systems in which social workers work (e.g., social welfare/social service) have not. The profession must continue to take the lead in bringing about change in these systems through the empowerment of people so they will be more responsive to the needs of racial and other oppressed groups.

B. This material is an essential part of an introductory social work/ social welfare course. Students can begin to examine and critically think about the impact of racism and discrimination on vulnerable groups within U.S. society had how these problems contribute to unmet human need. It is important that students become sensitive to and gain an understanding of these forces, so that they can be prepared to effectively intervene with these populations. Emphasis should be placed on the student gaining awareness of their own personal attitudes and values regarding racial and other diverse groups. Of particular importance is the students, understanding and acceptance of the human diversity perspective.

Students need to develop the following

1. An understanding of and sensitivity to the destructive forces of racism and discrimination and their impact on the vulnerable and disenfranchised groups who experience them.

2. An understanding of how racism and discrimination against persons from diverse groups in society affect their individual social functioning and contributes to their difficulties in meeting their human needs.

3. An understanding of the causes of racism and its history in the U.S.

4. An awareness of and sensitivity to the reactions of racial and other diverse groups to racism and discrimination, and their struggles to achieve equality and a sense of social justice within U.S. society.

5. An understanding of the responses made by the social welfare system and the social work profession to racism and discrimination.

6. An understanding of and sensitivity to the human diversity perspective.

7. An awareness of their own personal values and attitudes regarding racial and other diverse groups.

8. An understanding of how empowerment can be used as a strategy to assist oppressed groups.

C. The nature of the material lends itself well to student participation in useful classroom learning activities and class discussions. Instructors can be quite creative in the development of classroom learning experiences that will assist students in understanding the impact of racism and discrimination on special population groups. Direct "hands-on" learning experiences are perhaps most useful in assisting the students in learning this material. Most important, learning activities that focus on the student gaining an awareness of their personal values relative to these groups are most useful. The use of case material or examples is suggested in the teaching of this material.

Suggested learning activities.

1. To assist the students in beginning to understand the impact of discrimination on racial groups, the reactions of persons from these groups to it, and how social workers are faced with dealing with its effects, divide the class into groups and have them work with the following case examples.

Situation #1—A Native American man comes to the Social Services agency seeking financial assistance for his family. He is unemployed and has been for some time. He responds to the social worker assigned to his case in an angry, suspicious and defensive manner. The man demands to talk with the Native American social worker employed by your agency, who at the time is on vacation.

Situation #2—A 39-year-old Black man comes into your agency seeking assistance in finding employment and temporary financial assistance for his family. He has been laid off from his job as a meat cutter at the local packing plant and has had difficulty finding employment for about six weeks. His savings have been used up. He reacts to you in a suspicious and angry manner, saying: "No one will hire me because I'm Black. I think that's the reason I got laid off, too. The S.O.B. of a shift supervisor wanted to hire one of his white friends.,,, You get the impression that he thinks you are prejudiced too and won't help him.

The groups should discuss the following issues in relation to the above case situations:

1. What accounts for or would explain the initial reactions of persons from the case examples upon entering the agency for assistance?

2. How do you think these persons feel about seeking help from the agency? What potential areas of conflict do you think you would encounter in attempting to assist these persons?

3. How would you feel about these persons if you were the social worker assigned to assist them? Do any of their reactions arouse feelings within you? If so, what are they?

2. To assist the students in becoming aware of their personal values regarding persons from diverse groups within society and the kinds of value dilemmas faced by social workers in working with such persons, divide the class into 3 groups and give them the following case example. Each of the groups is assigned a different couple. Have them read the example and discuss in their groups the questions that follow the case example.

You (collectively) are an adoptions worker in an agency, and a couple has come in seeking to adopt a child. According to the rules under which your agency handles the social and legal aspects of the adoption process, any couple or single parent may adopt who is emotionally stable according to the discretion of the worker, is financially secure and able to provide an adequate home. You, as the worker, have a great deal of discretion under these rules, and the agency administration has made it clear that it will support your discretion.

One partner of the couple is a physician with a good income from ten years of practice in the community. The other is a college professor, has been employed at the local university for nine years, has gained tenure and has been promoted to chairperson of the biology department Their reason for wishing to adopt is that they feel they have a great deal of love to give a child, enough security to provide well, and would like to "complete,, their family with two or three children, adopted in intervals. It is obvious to you that they have a great deal of respect and affection for each other, and the home and future they might provide their children seems excellent.

Group #1—The husband is confined to a wheelchair as a result of a spinal cord injury some years earlier.

Group #2— The husband is Black, the wife is white. They have requested to adopt a Caucasian child.

Group #3—This is a lesbian couple.

Discuss in your group:

1 What feelings do you have as an individual about this couple?

2. What feelings as a group do you have about this couple?

3. What personal values do you have about this situation that might affect your judgment and decision about your couple's request?

4. What value conflicts do you think might occur between yourself, the couple, and the agency in your situation?

D. Class discussion or study questions

1. How have racism, prejudice and discrimination contributed to unmet human needs with U.S. society?

2. What are the differences between prejudice and discrimination? Is it possible for a person to be prejudiced, but not discriminate against persons from racial or diverse groups, or vise versa? Give examples.

3. What are the differences between individual and institutional racism? Give examples.

4. What do the value orientations of egalitarianism and individualism have to do with a person engaging in discrimination against racial and other diverse groups?

5. What do the factors—experience and interaction with persons from racial groups, geographical location, and learned responses through socialization—have to do with the development of prejudice and discrimination on a societal level?

6. Define and discuss the ideological factors involved in the causation of racism, assimilation, mutual assimilation, cultural pluralism.

7. What have been some of the resultant gains or losses that have been experienced by each of the predominant minorities of color through their individual civil rights movements?

8. What are the reasons to be optimistic about the problem of racism in contemporary society? What are reasons to be pessimistic?

9. What is the definition of ageism? What factors form the basis of discrimination against the elderly with U.S. society?

10. What societal attitudes, norms or values have contributed to the cause of sexism, discrimination toward women in U.S. society?

11. What is "homophobia,,? How has discrimination directed toward gays and lesbians contributed to the problems in social functioning they face?

12. Identify other diverse groups within U.S. society that are targets of discrimination. Give examples of the types of discrimination they face.

13. What efforts since the 1960s have been made by the profession of social work to address the problem/condition areas of racism and discrimination? What have professional organizations such as NASW and CSWE done to contribute to these efforts?

14. Define and discuss the human diversity perspective. What knowledge and skills do social workers need to effectively intervene with diverse groups?

15. In what ways should the profession empower disadvantaged and oppressed groups to bring about change in the social welfare/social service systems so they will be more responsive to their needs?

E. Objective (multiple choice) examination questions. Choose the *best* response.

1. Racism and discrimination toward diverse groups in U.S. society has:

   a. caused unmet human needs within these groups.

   b. denied these groups full access to resources necessary to sustain life.

   X c. both of the above

   d. brought about the passage of legislation that forbids discrimination and prejudice.

2 The process of prejudging persons on the basis of alleged or actual individual or group characteristics is:

   a. racism.

   d. discrimination.

   c. ethnocentrism.

   X d. prejudice.

3. The negative actions or behaviors of persons from majority society toward persons from racial groups is:

   a. ethnocentrism.

   X b. discrimination.

   c. prejudice.

   d. racism.

4. Institutional racism is manifested in:

    a. the actions or behaviors of individuals within the majority that discriminate against a person or persons from a minority group.

X b. the collective acts, attitudes, and behaviors of the majority society against a minority group as a whole.

    c. the actions of isolated individuals of the majority that discriminate against individuals from majority groups.

    d. societal structures that respect the values and culture of persons from minority groups.

6. A person holding the value orientation of egalitarianism would most likely:

    a. discriminate against persons from racial groups.

X b. not discriminate against persons from racial groups.

    c. would neither be prejudiced against nor discriminate against persons from racial groups.

    d. be unable to identify with the plight of racial groups.

7. The development of racial prejudice occurs as a result of:

    a. the presence of racial groups in particular geographical locations.

    b. experience or interact with them.

    c. learning of prejudicial attitudes transmitted through socialization processes within the majority culture.

X d. all of the above.

8. Which of the following ideologies views racism from a liberal perspective that contends that persons from racial groups should be able to maintain their racial heritage, yet share equally in the overall framework of society?

    a. ideology of assimilation

    b. mutual assimilation

X c. cultural pluralism

    d. melting pot assimilation.

9. Although some collective gains have been made by Blacks in their struggle to achieve equality through civil rights, they continue to experience:

    a. economic problems (poverty).

    b. inequality in educational systems.

    c. inequality in the employment market.

X d. all of the above.

10. A positive outcome in the struggle for Native Americans' civil rights has been:

   a. violent protest has shown that Native American peoples are no longer willing to live with the oppressions caused by U.S. racist attitudes.

X b. the federal government's lessening of control in Indian affairs, and engagement in the course of policy for self- determination for Native American people.

   c. Native Americans enjoy a better quality of life than ever before.

   d. lessening of discrimination and prejudice by majority group within the society.

11. Mexican Americans have made the most gains in achieving equality in:

   a. the employment market.

   b. the educational system.

X c. the political arena.

   d. the entertainment arena.

12. Asian Americans experience some difficulty in approaching and gaining access to human services due to:

   a. language and cultural barriers.

   b. they are passive and non-verbal.

   c. they are fearful and distrustful because of prior negative experiences with government.

X d. all of the above.

13. Mechanisms for dealing with ageist attitudes:

   a. should be focused on society at large.

   b. should be focused on social policies that negatively affect the elderly.

   c. can include lobbying and advocacy on behalf of this population.

X d. all of the above.

14. Although some progress has been made over the past two decades concerning women's rights, the most serious threats may arise from:

   a. economic recession.

X b. court decisions (e.g., abortion and reproductive rights, and affirmative action).

   c. intensified discriminatory practices toward women.

   d. minorities of color drawing attention away from women's rights issues.

15. The consequences for gays and lesbians of homophobic attitudes have been:
   a. blatant and open discrimination against them.
   b. some have internalized homophobic attitudes resulting in diminished self images.
   c. a view that the problems they experience are unique and are a result of their sexual life style.
X d. all of the above.
16. The human diversity perspective emphasizes which of the following relative to human characteristics and behavior?
   X a. differences rather than normalcy
   b. normalcy rather than differences
   c. skin color and biological differences
   d. cultural and social differences.
17. Social workers in operationalizing a human diversity perspective in practice with diverse groups should:
   a. assist persons to maintain their cultural integrity.
   b. remove the barriers to their full participation in society.
X c. both of the above.
   d. to assist person to give up their cultural ties so that they may assimilate into the mainstream of society.
18. In empowering disadvataged and oppressedgroups the activities of the social worker would be to:
   a. Identify the obstacles to power.
   b. Implement change strategy to eliminate or redirect the effects of the obstacles to power.
Xc. both of the above
   d. Give power to these groups at the expense of other groups.

Part II

Two Attributes of the Social Welfare System: Social Work and Fields of Practice

The social work profession has developed in concert with the social welfare system and has been greatly influenced by that system. Chapter 6 considers the emergence of the social work profession within social welfare by discussing the profession's historical roots and its contemporary nature. Social work practice and social service delivery are organized around problem/condition areas or around population groups (i.e., families and communities). Students learn about the complexity of service delivery in the social welfare system and develop an understanding of the functioning of the system by studying individual fields of practice. Students also learn about the scope of practice and differences between the fields. This information will help students make good choices about practice interests and career goals.

Chapters 7 through 14 offer detailed discussion of the fields of practice within the social welfare system. Several of the fields of practice examined are considered to be traditional, that is where social work has had considerable history of involvement. Also, a chapter is devoted to two developing fields of practice, industrial and rural. The final chapter in this part of the text re-examines concepts and issues that were introduced earlier as a way of analyzing how the service delivery system designed to meet human need has developed, and the methods employed by social workers in the delivery of services.

Chapter 6

The emergence of the social work profession within social welfare

Chapter 6 helps students gain an understanding to the historical emergence of social work as the primary profession within the social welfare system, the nature of and development of professional social work organizations and the development of professional education within higher education for social work. Students will also gain an awareness of and appreciation for the historical development of social work and its close ties to the development of the social welfare system. Students will be able to see social work come alive through the presentation of practice methods, and how practice is organized by various fields or practice.

A. Key points and issues

1 The precursors of the present social work system were the church and government agencies. The clergy of the early church were probably the first professionals to engage in a formalized assistance structure. Later, Poor Law authorities, acting under the provision of the English Poor Law, did so.

2. The roots of social work in the United States lie in the voluntary efforts of private philanthropic organizations and settlement houses. At the turn of the century, these groups sought to professionalize their activities and create a profession

3. The COS took an early step toward professionalization when it organized methods and procedures for doing charity work into what was later called "case work.,, Charity workers needed training to use these procedures appropriately. At first, training consisted of apprenticeships, but gradually a more formalized training—lectures, reading and discussion — evolved. Still later, the annual conference of the National Conference of Charities and Corrections provided training opportunities by acting as an exchange where ideas and work experiences of charity workers could be discussed. The settlement houses also organized training. This training consisted of formal lectures given to staff by professors from local colleges and universities.

49

4. Late in the 19th century, workers realized that more formal education, perhaps higher education, was needed to create a profession. Impetus for this effort was provided by the Dawes and Richmond papers, which culminated in the establishment of the first school of social work.

5. Since the turn of the century, social work's status as a profession has been questioned at several points, beginning with the work of Flexner in 1916, continuing from the 1920s through the 1940s and culminating with Greenwood's work in 1957. Though social work today is recognized by most authorities as a profession, this status continues to be questioned from time to time. Recently, two approaches for examining this issue have been presented: the "process model,,, as discussed by Leslie Leighninger; and the "power/control model," presented by Gary Lowe, Laura Rose Zimmerman, and P. Nelson Reid.

6. The development of professional organizations was critical to the professionalization of social work. This process began in a somewhat fragmented and piecemeal fashion. From the 1920s through 1950, seven separate professional social work organizations existed. In 1955, however, these organizations merged into a single organization—the National Association of Social Workers.

7. Another step toward the professionalization of social work was the emergence of education and training for the profession. The first educational programs consisted largely of agency training efforts. Later, professionals established programs of higher education and developed an accreditation process for professional education (CSWE, 1952).

In the 1960s and 1970s, social change and the revival of humanitarian values brought about considerable development of social welfare services and expansion of the formal delivery system; social work professionals "rediscovered,, the importance of social action. It also created a shortage of professionals qualified to deliver services. What resulted was a reduction in elitism within the profession, an opening of the profession to people with appropriate baccalaureate education, and a recognition of the BSW as the first professional degree. These trends have continued into the early 1990s.

8. Social work is difficult to define, and no single definition meets the needs of all within the profession. The most useful definitions are those offered by NASW discussed early in the chapter.

9. A basic criterion for a profession is that it possess a body of knowledge. The knowledge base of social work generally consists of: (1) knowledge borrowed from the natural and social-behavioral sciences; (2) knowledge developed from its own experiences in helping people (practice wisdom); and (3) knowledge developed through research. In today's world a social worker must possess a broad knowledge base that includes:

   a. knowledge of human behavior,

   b. knowledge about human relationships and interaction,

   c. knowledge of social work practice theory,

   d. knowledge about social policy and services, e. knowledge of self.

   f. specialized knowledge enabling the social worker to work with specific groups of people or particular practice situations.

10. Social work practice is guided by a set of values about human beings and the human condition. Social work's value base serves as an ethical guide for the social worker in day-to-day work. The text presents the basic social work values and a summary of the major principles of the social work code of ethics.

11. Social work practice is set in motion by a skill base that provides the social worker with the means by which to facilitate change. The skills that social workers use can be organized into three general skill-cluster areas: (1) interpersonal helping skills, (2) social work process skills, and (3) evaluation and accountability skills. Each area is described in the text.

12. As social work has evolved, a number of methods and approaches to social work practice have emerged. The first were the traditional methods of casework, group work, and community organization. In the later 1960s the integrative approach, consisting of the micro and macro methods, was developed. Later, the profession, as recognition was given to the BSW as the first professional degree, accepted the generalist method of social work. Today the generalist approach to practice is the forte of the BSW-level workers. MSW workers possess specialized and advanced knowledge and skill organized around problem/condition areas, specific fields of practice, or non-direct service methods such as social planning, community organization or administration.

13. The authors also present other professional requirements, largely focused on professional identification, including membership in NASW and professional licensing.

B. Students generally resist a consideration of historical materials. Yet, without an understanding of what has gone on before, students will be able to develop only a limited understanding of the present status of the profession. Instructors should help students recognize the importance of historical materials so that clear perceptions of social work can be acquired. The instructor's attitudes toward history and their enthusiasm in teaching such material is a crucial factor in developing positive attitudes among students.

Much of this material is designed to socialize the students within the profession and provide a background through which they might consider the roles and functions of social workers presented in the fields of practice section of this text.

Students need to develop the following.

1. A recognition that the historical development of the profession is closely related to the historical development of the formal social welfare system.

2. The understanding that, although the roots of social work as it emerged in the United States are in volunteerism, to progress the profession had to move away from volunteer activity to professional practice based on specialized knowledge and skills.

3. An awareness of efforts to establish social work as a profession through the development of professional education and the formation of a professional organization.

4. A sense that, although social work's status as a profession has been and continues to be questioned at times, social work is recognized as a profession that makes significant contributions to the fulfillment of human need and the improvement of people's social functioning.

5. An understanding that social work is a young profession that is still in transition. Social work is both a challenging and frustrating profession.

6. An understanding of the major issues or tensions that have challenged the social work profession .

7 An understanding of the essential components of social work's knowledge base.

8. An understanding of and sensitivity to the values of the profession and of how they are operationalized in practice through the code of ethics.

9. An understanding of the three skill-cluster areas of social work's skill base.

10. A basic understanding of the traditional methods of social work practice and the integrative approach to practice. It is particularly imperative that students understand the generalist method of practice.

11. An understanding of the professional requirements that exist for the various levels of social work practice. Students should also understand the purposes and missions of NASW and the importance of social work licensing.

12. An understanding of the nature of a field of practice.

Suggested learning activities

1. To assist students in seeing the relevancy of historical materials, understand the past struggles and efforts associated with the emergence of social work as a profession, and to understand how and under what circumstances the profession emerged, divide the class into groups and have them consider the following.

Assume that social work is just emerging today, as it did during the early 1900s.

   a. What efforts would be needed to accomplish this in today's world? Would these efforts be the same or different than the ones in which leaders engaged at the turn of the century? If different, what factors in the present would account for the differences?

   b. What efforts seemed to contribute to the emergence of the profession in the early 1900s? Would any of these efforts be helpful today?

2. It is our feeling that students have few opportunities to understand and appreciate the vast and rich history of the profession, in particular historical figures who have exemplified the vitality of social work through their contributions to the professions or to the general welfare of the United States. To enrich students, learning in this regard, we suggest the following be given to the students as a written assignment.

Students will write a bibliographical sketch on a prominent historical figure in social work. Students may select a person who has made contributions in one of the following areas:

    a. direct or indirect service or in the development of practice theory;

    b. enhancement of the profession through professional associations and/or social work education;

    c. Advancement of disadvantaged ethnic, racial, religious or socio-economic groups;

    d. development and implementation of policy and programs with national or regional implications

A good resource for this assignment is the *Encyclopedia of Social Work,* 18th edition, Vol. 2 J-Y and Bibliographies, 1987, which contains short biographic sketches on such historical persons. Require the students to engage in research on their historical person beyond what exists in the *Encyclopedia,* by examining the specific publications or other contributions made by the individual The *Encyclopedia will* lead the student to works where more information may be obtained on the person.

3. To help students understand current trends and issues associated with the profession, divide the class into groups and ask them to discuss and report orally to the class on the following.

    a. What events or circumstances brought about the recognition and sanction of the baccalaureate degree as the first entry level of professional practice?

    b. Do BSW practitioners assume the same or different roles as their MSW colleagues? What roles are the same, which are different?

    c. What arguments have been presented against the recognition of the BSW level as professional practice? What have been the arguments for the BSW level?

4. For the purpose of understanding what social work is, divide the class into groups and have each group review the NASW definition of social work and the working statement on the purpose of social work presented in Chart I of the chapter. Have them discuss the following points.

    a. What are the key elements of the NASW definition of social work? What is meant by enhancing or restoring people's capacity for social functioning and creating social conditions favorable to that goal?

    b. What are the key beliefs that social workers should hold as stated in the working statement on the purpose of social work?

    c. What are the objectives of social workers when they work with people according to the working statement? How do social workers achieve these objectives?

5. To assist the students in understanding how social work's knowledge base is utilized in practice, divide the class into groups and have them review the six parts of social work's knowledge base presented in the chapter. Assign pieces of case material with sufficient detail, so that each group may identify or speculate on what parts of the knowledge base the social worker used or could have used in intervening into the situation in the case example.

6. For the purpose of developing further understanding of and sensitivity to social work's value based and how it is operationalized in practice, divide the **class into groups and assign each** group of the values presented in the chapter. Have each group discuss:

   a. What does the group think the value means?
   b. Is the value realistic or do you think it is too idealistic or philosophical?
   c. How does the value guide the social worker in work with people? Does it promote and enhance the helping process or hinder it?
   d. How could the social worker operationalize the value in practice?
   e. Are there barriers to the social worker operationalizing the value?
   f. Is it important that the social worker's personal values be congruent with the value your group is discussing?

7. To assist students in developing an understanding of the generalist method of social work practice, divide the class into groups and have them review the case example provided in this chapter. Ask them to analyze and evaluate the social worker's use of the generalist method of practice by addressing the following points.

   a. What needs or problems are present in the case example that would call for a generalist approach to intervention?
   b. What kind of knowledge base did the social worker use in the case example that reflects use of the generalist method of practice?
   c. In what intervention activities did the social worker engage that illustrate use of the generalist method?

D. Class discussion or study questions

   1. Describe the close ties that the historical development of social work has with emergence1 of the formal social welfare system.

2. Social work emerged in the United States from a number of distinctive roots. Identify and discuss the contributions of each of the roots.

3. How did the structure of early education for social workers differ from today's structure? What events or factors led to the movement of social work education into the mainstream of higher education?

4. Why is formal education considered essential for the preparation of a professional social worker, when there are numbers of persons carrying the title social worker who do not possess a professional degree.

5. Why did so many separate social work professional organizations emerge in the 1900s? What factors or circumstances led to their merger into a single professional organization (NASW) in 1955?

6. Abraham Flexner in 1915 studied social work and concluded that it was not a profession. Social work leaders (e.g., Richmond, Brown, Hodson) argued against this contention. What were these arguments? How did they influence social work's professional status?

7. Greenwood, in 1957, conducted a study of social work and concluded that it is a profession. Why did Greenwood and Flexner reach opposite conclusions? Do the "Process model,, or the "Power/control model,, clarify this issue?

8. What events, circumstances, and studies led to the recognition of the baccalaureate degree as the first professional or entry-level for professional practice?

9. What arguments have been presented for and against the recognition of the BSW as a professional practitioner of social work?

10. Discuss reasons it is difficult to articulate a single **definition of social** work. Would a clear definition be useful? Why?

11. Discuss the differences and similarities between social work and social welfare. Why are these two concepts often confused with each other?

12. One of social work's missions is to improve people's social functioning. How and at what levels within society does social work attempt to accomplish this?

13. Why is a knowledge base an essential element for social work practice? How does a knowledge base enable the social worker to do their work?

14. What is the difference between theoretical knowledge and practice wisdom?

15. What are values and how do they differ from knowledge? Why is it important that social workers be aware of their own values, the values of the profession, and the values of those with whom they work?

16. How does the social work code of ethics serve as a guide for the social worker in their day-to-day practice?

17. What is meant by the statement that a social worker needs a repertoire (bag of tricks) of skills? How does use of these skills assist the social worker in bringing about change?

18. What are the three skill cluster areas that social workers use as discussed in the chapter? Give an example of each.

19. Discuss the generalist approach to social work practice. What is a generalist social worker? How is the generalist approach different from a specialist approach to practice?

20. In what ways can a social worker develop, identify with the profession? Do you think professional identity is necessary? Why?

E. Objective (multiple choice) examination questions. Choose the *best* response.

1. The historical forerunners of today's social workers were:

   a. clergy of the early church.
   b. lay groups (ladies of charity) within the church.
   c. public poor law authorities.
 X d. all of the above.

2. Social work in the United States had its earliest development in the late 1800s and early 1900s in:

 X a. charity organization societies and settlement houses.
   b. public institutions.
   c. public social welfare agencies.
   d. National Conference on Charities.

3. The earliest training and education procedures for social work consisted of:

 X a. apprenticeship (on-the-job training).
   b. formal academic training.
   c. formal agency training.
   d. a combination of academic and agency training.

4. Formal education for professional social workers within the mainstream of higher education first began at the:

    a. 2-year associate level.

    b. baccalaureate level.

X e. graduate level.

    d. post-graduate level.

5. The official accrediting organization for social work education today is:

    a. Association of Training Schools of Social Work. b. Association of American Universities.

    c. Association for Accreditation of Schools of Social Work.

X d. Council on Social Work Education.

6. In 1955 several separate organizations of social workers merged to form:

    a. The American Association of Social Workers

X b. The National Association of Social Workers.

    c. The National Conference of Social Welfare Workers.

    d. The National Social Work Exchange.

7. An important attribute of a profession according to Earnest Greenwood is:

    a. constitution and bylaws.

X b. code of ethics.

    c. operation regulations.

    d. articles for incorporation.

8. Social work today is considered a:

    a. semi-profession.

    b. trade or vocation.

X c. a profession.

    d. a para-profession.

9. The first professional educational degree recognized as the entry level for social work practice is:

    a. Associate degree.

X b. Bachelor of Social Work (BSW)

    c. Master of Social Work (MSW)

    d. Doctorate in Social Work (Ph.D. or DSW).

10. Social work is:

    a. a special kind of social agency.

    b. the same as social welfare.

X c. a profession concerned with enhancing people's social functioning.

    d. an approach to working with families.

11. The primary concern of the social worker is with:

   a. the environment.

X b. the person-environment interaction.

   c. the person. d. providing welfare assistance.

12. Social work's knowledge base consists of:

   a. borrowed knowledge from social-behavior sciences.

   b. knowledge gained by social workers in practice.

   c. knowledge gained through research.

X d. all of the above.

13. Practice wisdom is:

   a. knowledge that is scientifically tested.

   b. knowledge arrived at through research efforts. c. knowledge borrowed from other academic disciplines.

X d. knowledge developed form the experience of working with clients.

14. In a helping situation the social worker should be sensitive to:

   a. personal values.

   b. client values.

   c. community values.

X d. all of the above.

15. The social work code of ethics tells social workers:

   a. who to serve.

   b. when to terminate services.

X c. how to conduct professional relationships.

   d. what practice strategies to use in various case situations.

16. The skill-cluster of interpersonal helping skills includes which of the following.

   a. communication and listening skills

   b. helping relationship skills.

   c. interviewing and counseling skills

X d. all of the above.

17. Casework is a traditional method of social work practice that focused intervention on:

   a. groups of people.

X b. individuals and families

   c. communities.

   d. individuals, groups, families and communities.

18. The generalist social worker:

X a. begins intervention by assessing client needs and developing change strategy that will meet the need and solve client problems.

   b. fits particular methods of practice to assessment of client need.

   c. is a "jack of all trades.

   d. is a specialist in a particular area of practice.

19. The licensure of social workers:

X a. provides for sanction and public regulation of the profession.

   b. affects only private practitioners.

   c. is required for all social work positions.

   d. requires only those engaged in private practice to be licensed.

20. Fields of practice in social work are organized in which of the following ways:

   a. organized around a particular problem area.

   b. organized in host settings in which social workers are employed.

   c. organized around a particular population group. d. organized around a particular context, as with focus on a particular social system.

X e. all of the above.

Chapter 7

Income maintenance as a response to human need

This chapter assists students in understanding that an important function of the social welfare system is to provide financial assistance to people who, for whatever reason, temporarily or permanently lack sufficient income to meet their basic living needs. The students learn how public-governmental income maintenance services respond to the needs of such persons. Some of the material presented is historical. This information is critical to the development of an understanding of the societal values and philosophies and the economic and social changes that have influenced the development of the contemporary system of income maintenance services. The student will also become familiar with current programs of income maintenance, including: local, state, state-federal programs, food assistance programs; and housing programs and services. The strengths and inadequacies of these programs, as well as recent reforms in these programs are discussed.

Students also consider the role of social workers in the delivery of income maintenance programs and

A. Key points and issues

1. Income maintenance services are designed for the purpose of meeting the basic living needs of people who are unable to do so on their own. The services also maintain and control service delivery mechanisms and the extent to which these needs are met.

2. The primary goal of income maintenance services is to ensure that persons or groups of persons are able to live at a minimum level of subsistence and life satisfaction.

3. The current structure of income maintenance services in the United States has been influenced in its development by two major value perspectives. One value perspective speaks to society's humanitarian concerns; the other contends that deprived or disadvantaged persons are in some way responsible for their own conditions.

61

4. The structure of income maintenance services can be analyzed by examining the extent to which society assumes responsibility for people with unmet needs. A number of approaches to the structuring of income maintenance services are discussed: including the residual, the institutional, the developmental, industrialization, structural, societal obligation, social rights of people, the all-people (whatever government does it does for all) and the poor people. Each is discussed as to how it influences current income maintenance responses.

5. In order to understand the current system of income maintenance services, it is necessary to understand their historical background, including values, philosophies and motives that have shaped the structure of the system. The historical development of income maintenance services is discussed, beginning with the old world background and continuing with their history in the United States.

6. All levels of government—local, state and federal—are involved in providing income maintenance programs. These programs are designed to provide income to people whose other income is insufficient to meet their needs. The programs are referred to as income transfers in that they transfer or distribute income resources collected by various levels of government through taxation to the recipients of income maintenance programs.

7. Current income maintenance programs consist of: local programs (e.g., general assistance), federal-state programs (AFDC) and federal programs (SSI). Food assistance programs are also available (e.g., food stamps), as well as other federal programs designed to provide assistance to special populations (e.g., veteran's pensions and BIA general assistance for Native Americans living on reservations). Each of these programs has strengths, limitations and criticisms associated with it.

8. The work ethic has strongly influenced the income maintenance system in the U.S. There has been a historical relationship between work and welfare in the structure and policy of the system. This historical relationship is discussed with identification of work experience programs that have developed (e.g., WIN, Community Work Experience Program (CWEP), commonly known as "Workfare," and most recently the Job Opportunities and Basic Skills Training Program (JOBS) created by P.L. 100-485, the Family Support Act of 1988).

9. For the last 25 years, alternatives to the current programs have been a source of concern for both the general public and social policy makers. Social change, economic cycles and the debate over values relative to whom should be helped and at what levels and expense have pushed the social welfare system toward "welfare reform.,, Two major reform proposals, the Family Assistance Plan in 1969 and the Jobs and Income Security Program 1977, were introduced to Congress but failed to become policy. A major overhaul of the AFDC Program occurred in 1988 with the passage by Congress of P.L. 100-485, the Family Support Act. The major provisions of which are highlighted in the text.

10. There is a relationship between inadequate income supports, poverty and housing problems. The lack of safe, affordable housing, combined with inadequate income and a lack of programs to assist low-income families have caused a housing crisis for many families.

11. Societal concern for meeting human needs through the provision of financial assistance was responsible for the emergence of social work as a profession. As the profession continued to evolve, other areas of human need captured its attention and the direct involvement of professionally-trained social workers in income maintenance services has gradually declined over the years. However, social work remains the largest profession in the public welfare sector. Large numbers of social workers are employed in public social service agencies. In recent years there has been a growing trend for BSWs to assume direct service positions in income maintenance services and this will likely expand due to the Family Support Act. Some MSWs also remain in this field of practice, assuming such roles as administrators, supervisors and program planners.

B. Teaching this material may be somewhat difficult because, again, some of the material is historical. The instructor's enthusiasm in teaching this material is an essential key in motivating and guiding students in the learning of these materials. Income maintenance services should be seen as a legitimate field of social work practice. This is particularly germane in the arena of undergraduate education, as there is great potential for the utilization of BSW practitioners in the provision of newly created services. This will further open career opportunities for them in the profession.

The student should develop the following.

1. An understanding that income maintenance services should enable individuals and families to live at an adequate level of subsistence and life satisfaction.

2. An awareness of and sensitivity to the values perspectives that have influenced the development of income maintenance services and currently have an impact on their structure and delivery. Students should particularly understand the issues of social control that have the potential of putting at a disadvantage persons the system is designed to assist.

3. An understanding of the approaches by which society assumes responsibility for people with unmet needs, and how each has influenced the current income maintenance response. These are: the residual, institutional and developmental, industrialization, structural, societal obligation-social rights, all-people (whatever government does it does for all) and the poor people approaches.

4. An understanding of the history of the development of income maintenance services and how the past contributes to the current structure of the system.

5. An understanding of the current programs of income maintenance, who delivers them, how they are funded, who they assist, their advantages and disadvantages, and their criticisms.

6. An understanding of the history of the relationship between work and welfare. ability to identify the major work experience programs.

7. An understanding of and the ability to critically analyze the recent reforms in the current system of income maintenance services.

8. Understanding of the major contributors to and the impacts of the low-cost housing shortage in the U.S.

9. An understanding of social work's involvement in the provision of income maintenance services, the roles assumed by social workers and the potential for further involvement in the future.

C. Suggested learning activities

1. Invite a social worker employed in a public agency that provides income maintenance services to speak to the class about their work in this field.

2. If possible, arrange for the class or separate groups of students

to take a field trip to a public welfare agency for the purpose of learning the services they provide and to interact with individuals who deliver the services. Have the students orally report to the class on this experience.

3. If possible arrange for the class or groups of students to visit an emergency shelter for the homeless. Have them interview the staff to learn first-hand what the problems are, what services are available and what barriers exist to service delivery.

4. For the purpose of assisting students in developing insights into some of the issues, values and philosophies that have had an impact on the delivery of income maintenance services, divide the class into several groups and assign each group one or more of the following discussion questions. Have them make a oral report to the class on their discussion.

a. Discuss the issue of individual versus governmental responsibility for meeting human needs. Who is responsible? What roles through the provision of income maintenance services should government assume in meeting human needs? When, if ever, does individual responsibility end?

b. What are the stereotypic views and criticisms of "welfare', held by society? Are they more negative than positive? Are any supported by empirical evidence or research? What can be done to overcome the negative ones? Support your responses by giving reasons.

c. What are the differences and similarities between approaches to income maintenance discussed in the text? How has each influenced the manner in which services are provided?

d. Should recipients of welfare be required to work? Are current work experience programs designed more to reduce poverty or to reduce welfare dependency?

e. Should the provision of welfare support be the right of every citizen of the United States? Support your response with reasons.

f. Are the current reforms in welfare going to be sufficient and long lasting? Or are other reforms likely to be needed in the future.

g. Discuss the advantages and disadvantages of localized control over income maintenance programs. Why might one argue for centralized federal control of these programs? Give reasons to support your response.

5. Provide a piece of case material in which a family lacks suffi-

cient income to meet their needs. Divide the class into groups and ask them to assess the family's needs and identify the potential income maintenance services that could be provided to this family. Ask them to support their choices out of their understanding of the various income maintenance programs.

Class discussion or study questions

1. Define income maintenance. Also, what is meant by the statement: income maintenance services are designed to meet the basic living needs of people unable to meet them on their own, while controlling the extent to which the needs are met?

2. Are income maintenance services guaranteed to all persons by law? If so, under what circumstances are individuals and families entitled to receive such services?

3. Discuss the notion that the current income maintenance programs in the United States are based on two major value perspectives. What are the two values perspectives? How has each contributed to the development and structure of the current programs?

4. Are the current approaches to income maintenance services more residual, institutional, or developmental, industrial, structural, societal obligated, all-people, or poor people oriented in terms of organization and delivery.

5. Why is the English Poor Law of 1601 considered the foundation of the U.S. system of social welfare and income maintenance?

6. What has been the influence of the Protestant work ethic on the organization and structure of income maintenance programs?

7. Discuss the local program of income maintenance, known as general assistance. How is it funded? What are its disadvantages?

8. What are the major criticisms of the AFDC program? Are the criticisms valid? If so, Why? If not, why aren't they? How will the provisions of the Family Support Act of 1988 affect the public's view of the AFDC program.

9. What factors have contributed to the housing crisis for low income families in contemporary society? What new services are needed to address this problem?

10. What were the factors associated with the failure of the Family Assistance Plan and the Jobs and Income Security Program to become law? Why weren't these factors an influence in the recent passage of the Family Support Act?

11. Discuss work experience programs. What have been the advantages and disadvantages of these programs?

12. What are the roles that social workers assume in the current income maintenance services delivery system? Should social workers be more involved in the delivery of these services?

E. Objective (multiple choice) examination questions. Choose the *best* response.

1. Income maintenance is a means by which income:
   a. is maintained at a societally defined level.
   b. is controlled at some defined level.
   c. is provided to meet the basic living needs of persons unable to do so on their own.
   X d. all of the above.

2. The value influencing the organization and structure of income maintenance services that contends that persons who are poor, deprived or disadvantaged in some way are responsible for that condition is:
   a. humanitarian concern.
   X b. blaming the victim.
   c. punishing the victim.
   d. controlling the victim.

3. The institutional approach to income maintenance is based on the assumption that:
   a. income maintenance should be provided only when the natural channels of family and market economy fail to do so.
   b. society has no responsibility to provide for those unable to support themselves.
   X c. in an industrialized society, income maintenance should be the first-line responsibility of such a society.
   d. income maintenance is provided to assist persons at defined points in the life cycle to prevent problems of inadequate income.

4. The motivation for persons being helpful to one another as human societies began was based on:

X a. mutual aid for protection and survival.
  b. public law.
  c. religious expectations.
  d. economic concerns.

5. The complete shift of responsibility for poor relief in England in 1601 from the churches to government came with the legislation known as:

  a. Act for the Punishment of Sturdy Beggars and Vagabonds.
  b. Statute of Laborers.
  c. Henrican Poor Law.
X d. English Poor Law.

6. The legislative foundation for our present system of income maintenance services is:

  a. The New Federalism.
  b. The New Deal.
X c. the Social Security Act of 1935.
  d. The Income Security Act.

7. The original programs of old-age assistance, aid to the disabled and aid to the blind were combined into a single, federally-administered program known as:

  a. Selected Security income.
X b. Supplemental Security income
  c. State supported income.
  d. Service supported income.

8. The work experience program, attached to the AFDC program authorized by the Family Support Act of 1988 is:

  a. a work incentive program, (WIN).
  b. a comprehensive employment and training act, (CETA).
X c. Job Opportunities and Basic Skills Training Program (JOBS).
  d. Community Work Experience Program ("Workfare',).

9. Which one of the following is not a characteristic of today's income maintenance programs:

  a. provide a social control function.
X b. eligibility is based on universal provision.
  c. eligibility is based on categorical provision.
  d. provide a safety net for persons whose needs go unmet.

10. A major overhaul of the AFDC program occurred in 1988 with the passage of:

   a. Welfare Reform Act.

   b. Omnibus Budget Reconciliation Act.

X e. Family Support Act.

   d. Family Assistance Plan.

11. The single most contributing factor to the problem of homelessness as identified by the text

   a. unemployment.

   b. increase in single parent households with low income.

X c. the lack of available affordable housing, combined with a lack of income resources to rent available affordable housing.

   d. welfare dependence.

12. A role performed by social workers n the provision of income maintenance services is:

   a. direct services role in income maintenance.

   b. administrator.

   c. researcher.

   d. program planner.

X e. all of the above.

Chapter 8

Child welfare services

This chapter assists students to gain an understanding of the broad field of social work practice known as child welfare. The content of the chapter focuses on needs of children for care and protection in contemporary U.S. society and the programs and services provided by the social welfare and social services delivery systems needed to insure children's well-being. Students are exposed to the broad array of services that are provided by both public and private social services agencies to children, and the values, philosophies and social policy issues that have an impact on the delivery of services to this special population. Students will also understand the roles and functions of social work in the delivery of services to children. Case material is provided to help students understand the scope and nature of social work practice in child welfare services so that they may consider this field of practice as a possible career choice.

A. Key points and issues

1. Child welfare services are a series of activities and programs that express society's special concern for children and its willingness to assume responsibility for some children until they are unable to care for themselves.

2. Much of the focus in child welfare services has been on addressing the needs of children when their families functioning, particularly that of the parent, has jeopardized their well-being. The key to providing for the needs and well-being of children is to support and strengthen families. The social welfare/social welfare services delivery system recognizes the importance of the family for the child.

3. The child welfare service system provides two broad areas of service: services to insure the child's maintenance within their families and services to children unable to remain in their own homes. Services in the first area include: day care, nutrition, income maintenance, mental health, family preservation services, educational and school social work and services to adolescent parents. Services in the second area include: family foster

care, institutional treatment, community-based treatment, services such as group homes and residential care and adoption services.

4. The history of child welfare programs is extensive as the protection and care of children is considered one of the oldest forms of charity. To understand today's system of services to children, it is necessary to understand the historical events and trends that have shaped its development.

5. Currently, the emphasis in the provision of child welfare services is within a permanency framework, that is service provision designed to ameliorate the problem conditions that may jeopardize the well-being of children within their families so that children can remain in or be returned to their natural homes. Protective and family preservation services have this as their basic mission: for children unable to remain in their natural homes, substitute care services (foster care, institutional and adoption services) are provided with a permanency framework to create conditions of permanency in the lives of children.

6. Economic security for children and low-income families remains a stubborn and persistent problem. Recent research reports that children's poverty rates have increased steadily since 1970.

7. The social problems/conditions of physical abuse/neglect, emotional abuse/neglect and sexual abuse have reached crisis proportions, complicated by significant increases in the rate of reporting, overwhelming child protection agencies who have limited resources to investigate and intervene.

8. Other problems such as children born addicted to drugs, Fetal Alcohol Syndrome (FAS) or Fetal Alcohol Effect (FAE) have come to the forefront as significant problems for children. Health care for children is also of concern, due to the growing numbers of families who are without private or public health care insurance.

9. Families and children in today's world have complex needs and varying abilities to cope and meet the demands in living placed on them by society. Unmet need, or the inability to cope and meet these demands, may cause family dysfunction and a need for society to intervene via social welfare/social services to restore and strengthen the family as a social unit. Services such as day care services, homemaker/home health services, school/educational, family counseling, adolescent sexuality services to adolescent parents all have this mission as their primary purpose.

10. Currently, several trends and issues have an impact on the nature and scope of adoption services to children, including a new perspective relative to children who should be considered adoptable, including special-needs children and families who are deemed capable of adopting children. This area of service within the framework of permanency planning for children has provided increased opportunities for children to have a permanent home.

11. In the past and presently, the profession of social work has been involved in the delivery of child welfare services. The field of child welfare services is one of the most demanding but professionally rewarding fields of practice. Over the past decade, public child welfare agencies have lacked professionally-trained social workers. Response has been made to this by a number of national professional organizations who have begun collaborative efforts to advocate for adequate competent staff and other mechanisms such as worker certification. Training stipends have been made available.

B. Students tend to have considerable interest in this field of practice. Because of its broadness, more career opportunities are usually available than in most other fields of practice within the social welfare system. Therefore, students will likely take a keen interest in learning the materials presented in this chapter. The instructor, however, needs to be cautious and attempt to point out the realities of demand associated with this field, particularly those involving protective services, which is the most demanding and emotionally exhausting field of social work practice.

The student should develop the following.

1. Ability to define child welfare services from broad and narrow perspectives.

2. The recognition that much of the focus of child welfare services should be placed on supporting and strengthening the family as a social unit.

3. An understanding of the scope of child welfare services, with particular familiarity of the two broad areas of service and the individual areas of services provided in each.

4. Knowledge of the historical development of the child welfare field of practice.

5. An understanding of the permanency planning framework for services to children and how all child welfare services today have this as their basic goal.

6. An understanding of the problem/condition areas that jeopardize the well-being of children (e.g., child abuse, neglect and sexual abuse) and how, through the provision of services, these can be ameliorated.

7. An understanding that living in our society places some children and families at risk for unmet needs and family dysfunction. Students should become familiar with the wide array of in-home services that are available to assist children and families when problems occur.

8. Awareness of current concerns and problems within the child welfare field.

9. An understanding of substitute care services and their goals and missions within the permanency planning framework.

10. An understanding that social work practice opportunities within this **field are** vast and rewarding but also challenging, frustrating and demanding.

C. A variety of teaching methods would be useful in presentation of this material. There is a wealth of audio visual materials (e.g., film strips, slide presentations, audio tapes, video tapes and films) that have been produced related to the various services within this field of practice. The authors also believe that providing students with an opportunity to interact with community professionals working in the field is a useful learning activity that will help students understand the practicalities and realities associated with practice within the field of child welfare services. The use of case examples and materials will also assist the students in gaining experiential understandings relative to how social workers deliver services to children and families.

Suggested learning activities

1. Contact a number of community practitioners who provide several of the services to children discussed in the text and ask them to be involved in a panel presentation to the class on service delivery to children. Have each discuss their role and the services they provide and allow time for student questions and reactions.

2. As an alternative to assignment number 1, pair together students who are interested in a particular problem/condition affecting children (e.g., child abuse, adolescent sexuality services, children with disabilities, etc.) and have them interview community social workers who provide services to children

experiencing such problems. The focus of the interviews should be on the roles performed and services provided by the social workers. Have the student pairs present the information gained in the interview in class through an oral report.

3. Group research term paper. Students will work in groups (no more than 3 or 4 students per group) and collaboratively write a 10 to 15 page term paper on a problem/condition affecting children or area of services provided to children. The paper should cover the following points:

   a. overview and description of the problem/condition or service area.
   b. social policy issues affecting the funding and mechanisms for service delivery.
   c. identification and discussion of the social programs and social services delivered to deal with the problem/conditions experienced by children.
   d. identification of the roles and functions of social workers in the delivery of services to children .

Expect the students to use supportive literature or interviews with social workers and to cite their sources throughout the paper. Require a bibliography of sources of literature used in the writing assignment.

4. Provide the class with a piece of case material, or use the case example from the text, and develop an experiential learning activity on which groups of students in the class may work. The case material should contain sufficient detail on the problem situation, the services delivered and the intervention activities in which the social worker engaged. Ask the students to address the following relative to the case material:

   a. What are the problems the children and families face in the example that necessitate intervention?
   b. What appear to be the causes associated with the problem (e.g., individual, family, community, environmental)?
   c. What services could be provided that would likely ameliorate the problems in the situation?
   d. What specific roles and functions did or should the social worker perform relative to intervention into the problem-situation involved in the case?

3. What social policy or legal issues may have an impact on the plan for intervention and the services delivered in this case?

D. Class discussion or study question

1. Define child welfare service in both broad and narrow terms. Give examples of both broad child welfare services and specific areas of service.

2. Discuss the statement "the key to maintaining the well-being of children is to support and strengthen the family as a social unit.,, How does the social welfare/social services delivery system attempt to go about doing this?

3. What are the two broad areas of services within the scope of child welfare services? **Give** examples of specific services that are provided in each.

4. What is the permanency planning framework for services to children? How do both broad areas of child welfare services come into play in the development of permanency planning?

5. Discuss the responses made to the needs and problems of children under mutual aid and poor law arrangements. Were these responses based on a children's rights value or perspective, or more based on preventing a life of poverty for children and promoting self-sufficiency among children?

6. Discuss the efforts of the private-voluntary organizations in "child saving,, in the 1800s. Who was Charles Loring Brace, and what did he contribute to these efforts? Why is this system of care considered the forerunner of today's system of foster care for children?

7. What effect did the first White House Conference on children have on changing service delivery to children in the early 1900s?

8. What factors or events brought about the emergence of the U.S. Children's Bureau in 1912? Were the first efforts of the Bureau all that effective in promoting service delivery to children? How did the Sheppard-Towner Act of 1921 bolster the efforts of the U.S. Children's Bureau?

9. How has the Social Security Act of 1935 formed the basis of the public social service delivery system for children? What are the programs and services provided under the act that assist in meeting the needs of children and deal with the problems children experience?

10. What problems continue to be experienced by children from minority groups? Has the situation improved for some minority children? Which ones and in what ways?

11. What concerns and problems have recently emerged within the child welfare field?

12. How has the Adoptions Assistance and Child Welfare Reform Act of 1980, P.L. 96-272, contributed to the development of the permanency planning framework in child welfare services?

13. What are the basic aims of child protective services? Is the focus of concern more on protecting the children or on remedying the problems in family functioning which necessitate intervention, or both?

14. What are the three broad areas of interacting situational factors that appear to precipitate physical abuse and neglect? Is any one of these factors sufficient in and of itself to cause child abuse or neglect? If not, why is this so?

15. What is involved in the sexual abuse of children? What appear to be its causes?

16. What are the treatment approaches used and the **roles assumed by social workers in protect**ing children from physical abuse, neglect and sexual abuse?

17. Identify and discuss the other services that are designed to assist children in their own homes.

18. Why, when and for what reasons do children become in need of substitute care services?

19. Identify and discuss the specific areas of service in substitute care. Discuss how each is provided within the permanency planning framework.

20. The adoption of children services three main purposes. Identify and discuss each.

E. Objective (multiple choice) examination questions. Choose the *best* response.

1. Child welfare services are:

a. services provided by society to some children until such time as they can care for themselves .

b. any service that enables a child to develop fully and function effectively in society.

c. services provided to children and families when parental functioning has broken down, or when the child's developmental, emotional, or behavioral functioning jeopardizes his/her ability to remain within the family.

X d. all of the above.

2. Which of the following is an area of service within the broad area of substitute care givers?

  a. protective services

X b. family foster care.

  c. adolescent sexuality services

  d. homemaker/home health services.

3. Day care services, homemaker service, health care services, nutrition services, income maintenance services and family preservation services are all types of services provided within:

  a. substitute care services.

  b. protective services.

X c. services to children in their homes.

  d. public child welfare system.

4. The number one option in the permanency planning framework of child welfare services:

X a. work with natural family to ameliorate problematic conditions so the child may remain within the family home.

  b. placement with relatives.

  c. adoption placement.

  d. long-term foster care.

5. Orphaned and dependent children under the provisions of the colonial and later state poor laws were responded to in which of the following ways:

  a. received "outdoor relief,' — assistance provided directly to the family.

  b. placed in the institutions (almshouses).

  c. apprenticed or indentured to families so they could learn a trade or skill and become self-sufficient.

X d. all of the above.

6. The first White House Conference on Children contributed to a shift in priorities and policies relative to the care and protection of children by advocating for which one of the following:

  a. all children need a stable home environment.

  b. resources and services should be directed toward the maintenance of children in their own homes .

  c. the needs of children can be met best within the natural family with supportive help and resources .

  d. children should not be removed from their homes solely on the basis of inadequate family income .

X e. all of the above.

7. The current poverty rate for children Is

    a. stable, no significant changes have been experienced in recent years.

    b. at the lowest rate it has been for several years.

X c. has increased significantly since 1970.

    d. is leveling off and showing signs of decline.

8. The Indian Child Welfare Act of 1978 has had an impact on child welfare services for Native American children in which of the following ways.

    a. Native American tribes are afforded the right to intervene into child welfare matters that affect children enrolled in their tribe.

    b. tribes have the right to assume legal jurisdiction over Indian children and provide plans for their care.

    c. provides Native American people a measure of self- determination relative to the care of their children.

X d. all of the above.

9. A problem of current concern in the field of child welfare services is:

    a. economic security for children.

    b. permanency planning for children.

    c. child abuse and neglect.

    d. fetal alcohol syndrome and effect.

    e. the deprofessionalization of child welfare services.

X f. all of the above.

10. Which of the following problem/conditions affecting children would necessitate the intervention of child protective services?

    a. physical abuse/neglect

    b. emotional abuse/neglect

    c. sexual abuse

X d. all of the above

11. The primary emphasis of child protective services is to:

X a. modify social conditions and problems in parental functioning so as to allow the child to remain with the natural family.

    b. to immediately remove children from their homes when problems in parental functioning are occurring.

    c. to make sure that parents who are not providing for their children or are harming them in some way are prosecuted to the full extent of the law. d. to place abused and neglected children for adoption.

12. Child abuse and neglect reporting laws mandate that which one of the following report suspected incidences of abuse and neglect:

   a. general public

X b. selected professionals.

   c. victimized children.

   d. all of the above.

13. Which of the following has been found to be more prevalent and more damaging to children over extended periods of time:

   a. sexual abuse.

   b. physical abuse.

X c. physical-emotional neglect or abuse.

   d. abandonment of children by parents.

14. The role of social workers in child protective services is to:

   a. insure the on-going protection of the child or children.

   b. preparation and implementation of an interventive plan that assists the family to overcome the conditions or solve the problems that necessitated the intervention and place the child or children at risk.

X c. both of the above.

   d. insure that parents who abuse or neglect their children are arrested.

15. Social workers employed within the educational system perform which of the following roles:

   a. mediate at the point where students, parents and the community interface with each other.

   b. intervene into problems that jeopardize the child's educational experience. c. provide individual, family and group counseling services.

   d. assist school administrations with policy formation and planning for educational needs.

X e. all of the above.

16. The primary role for the social worker in working with adolescent parents is to:

X a. assist them in making decisions relative to the future of the unborn child.

   b. provide abortion counseling, sexuality counseling and family planning services.

   c. assist the client in making arrangements for the adoption of the child.

   d. provide economic assistance to the unmarried parent(s).

17. Social workers in working with family foster care situations perform which of the following roles:

   a. assist foster parents and children with adjustment and provide other supportive services.
   b. engage in permanency planning for the child's future.
   c. work with natural parents toward unification of children and parents.
X d. all of the above.

18. The new perspective relative to what children should be considered to adoptable is that:

   a. only infants should be placed for adoption.
   b. only order or handicapped children should be placed for adoption.
X c. any child in need of a permanent home should be considered adoptable.
   d. only children from racial groups or mixed-race decent should be placed.

19. Which of the following family types is considered a suitable resource for adoptive placement?

   a. childless couples
   b. single-parent families
   c. foster families
   d. families from racial groups
X e. all of the above

20. The role of social work in adoption services is which of the following:

   a. preparing children and families for adoptive placement. b. adoptive home finding.
   c. completing adoption home studies.
   d. providing supportive services to adoptive families with children in placement
X e. all of the above.

Chapter 9

Health care and social welfare

This chapter introduces students to the U.S. system of health care as a field of practice within social work ad as an area of human service within the social welfare system. The material in this chapter will assist students in understanding the broadness of the health care delivery system and how it attempts to meet the health care needs of individuals and families in U.S. society. Students should also come to understand the relationship between health care and social welfare and that some social welfare health care programs are designed to provide health care for persons who lack the necessary financial resources to purchase needed services within the open health care services delivery market. Students should understand the roles and functions of social work within the health care delivery system. Case examples are provided to illustrate the roles performed by social workers in the delivery of health care services. Finally, students are exposed to social policy issues that have shaped and will continue to have an impact on the delivery of health care services within the social welfare system.

A. Key points and issues

1. A common theme of health care and social welfare is that both systems are concerned with the whole person. This includes the bio-psycho-social and spiritual aspects of living and functioning.

2. Both systems are concerned with the impact of environmental factors as they relate to the health and social functioning of individuals and families.

3. Both systems also share a concern for the family. The health care system is concerned with the impact of family relationships on the patient and the impact of a patient's illness on the family system; the social welfare system is concerned with meeting unmet human needs caused by illness and disability, so as to improve the social functioning of individuals and the family. The health care and social welfare systems include various institutions that serve the individual and family.

83

4. The arrangements that have been used to deliver social welfare services have also been involved in the delivery of health care services.

5. The current health care services delivery system is a two-tier system. One tier of services for those who can afford to pay and another for those unable to pay.

6. The relationship between the health care system, the social welfare/social services delivery system and the social work profession has a long-standing history extending back as far as the later 1800s. Social work was introduced into hospitals in the early 1900s and those institutions have employed such workers from that time forward. In the 1930s social workers became recognized as health care professionals, as evidenced by the emergence of a professional organization for medical social workers. During the 1960s and 1970s, the role of the social worker in health care continued to expand, due largely to the implementation of the Medicaid and Medicare programs in 1965. These programs require the availability of social services to recipients. Other accreditation requirements of health care facilities have also contributed to the expansion of involvement of social work in the delivery of health care services since the 1970s.

7. The health care system can be divided into three major parts: the hospital, the long-term care facility and the community setting. The health care system is a multi-disciplinary professional setting employing various health care professions, including social workers. Social workers perform various roles in all three major components of the system.

8. Many social policy issues confront today's health care system. Recent changes in social welfare-health care policy (e.g., Medicaid and Medicare) related to limits on coverage (DRGs) have brought new concerns to the profession. No social problem is receiving more attention currently than the cost of health care, which is at a crisis. Significant numbers of individuals and families have no health care protection in the form of private, employer-sponsored, or public supported health insurance. Several proposals have emerged recently to respond to this problem. Social workers must continue to advocate for equity and equality in health care services delivery.

9. Social workers must also be concerned with preservation of

quality of life as medical technology advances, preventative health care, assuring appropriate health care in the diverse cultures and life-styles of Americans, and responding effectively to the AIDS crisis. Lastly, and of critical concern to all the above, is the issue of social worker's on-going role within the health care services delivery system.

B. The student should develop the following.

1. The understanding that the health care system, the social welfare system and the social work profession share a concern for meeting the health care needs of individuals and families and are linked together in a service delivery system that attempts to meet these needs.

2. An understanding of the definition of the health care system as presented in the text.

3 An understanding of the historical development of social legislation and policy relating to health care and social welfare/ social services in health care, and its impact on the structure and delivery of health care programs and services.

4. An understanding of the major approaches for change in health care funding currently being discussed, including understanding of the strengths and limitations of each.

5. An understanding of the historical development of social work in the health care system and the events and factors that have contributed to health care as a field of practice within the profession.

6. An understanding of the three major components of the contemporary health care system and the roles social workers perform in each of the components.

7. An understanding of how working in a host setting affects the practice of social work.

8. An understanding of the social policy issues that have an impact on the delivery of health care services, affect the roles and functions of social workers within the system, and have an impact on meeting health care and social functioning needs of individuals and families in contemporary U.S. society.

C. This field of practice offers broad and exciting career opportunities for social workers. The instructor's enthusiasm in the presentation of the materials in the chapter, as well as the use of supplemental materials and personal experiences, will motivate students to consider this field of practice as a possible career choice. As with most fields of practice, student/practitioner interaction is most helpful in increasing the student's learning and understanding of this field. Students would gain a great deal from guest lecturers who are practitioners in the health care field and can speak to the class on their work and other issues relative to the delivery of health care services. Using case materials and experiential learning activities is also a way to increase students' understanding of the needs of individuals and families for health care, health care programs and services available to them, social policies that affect service delivery, and the roles performed by social workers in the delivery of health care services.

Suggested learning activities.

1. Divide the class into groups and provide them with a case example with sufficient information to enable them to evaluate the above. You may want to use the examples provided in the text. Have the students address the following relative to the case example:

   a. assessment of the individual's or family's needs for health care services.

   b. health care programs or services that could be delivered to meet the needs in the situation.

   c. social policy or other issues that are involved in the delivery of health care services and that would affect service delivery in the example.

   d. the roles that were performed or could be performed by the social worker involved in the case example. Are there limitations on the roles that the social worker could perform, e.g., social work practice in a host setting?

2. To increase the students, understanding of social policy or other issues involved in health care and social welfare, divide the class into groups and assign one or more of the following issues to them for discussion:

   a. Is health care a right or privilege for individuals or families?

   b. Relative to the issue of quality of life, what bio-medical ethical questions are involved in making decisions about the right to live or die?

   c. Is the present system of health care services more preventative oriented or treatment and cure oriented? Should the system be more preventative oriented?

   d. How have social workers responded to the AIDS crisis? What should social workers be doing to ensure that AIDS victims receive equitable and quality services?

e. What should be the relationship between various health care professionals? Which professions should carry out which tasks relative to the delivery of health care services?

f. What different roles and tasks do MSWs and BSWs working the health care system assume? Is there a need for more effective utilization of the BSW social worker in the health care system?

3. To assist students in understanding the crisis in health care costs and the proposals being considered to respond to it, ask the students to participate in the following activity.

The American public often disagrees on what should be considered the role of government in matters such ;as social welfare and health care. Philip Popple and Leslie Leighninger, in their book *Social Work, Social Welfare and American Society* have offered as a framework for analysis, three competing views on the role of government in the economy and in the lives of people. They are: the conservative, liberal and radical. The conservative view calls for a "hands off policy," that government activity would pose a threat to the smooth functioning of a free market economy. Liberals contend that economic systems are imperfect and can be corrected by government intervention, which is justified and desirable. Radicals believe that government involvement in the economy is oppressive and produces inequity and inequality for certain groups in society, thus, a complete restructuring is necessary to produce equity in the distribution of economic resources.

Divide the students into three groups. Assign each of the groups one of the proposals for funding health care services; the private market approach, the employer-based approach and the government-based approach. Based on the descriptions of these proposals in the text (the instructor may want to supplement this with other materials on these proposals), have the students discuss the following

1. Does the approach your group is discussing appear to be more representative of the conservative, liberal or radical view of governmental involvement? Why do you think so?

2. What do you think the changes are that the proposal your groups is discussing will become public health care policy through legislative process? What reasons do you have that support your thinking?

3. What suggestions would your group make that you think would strengthen the proposal your groups is discussing?

Have a spokesperson from each group give a brief oral report to the class regarding each group's discussion of their assigned proposal. Follow this by open discussion questions and comment by the entire class.

D. Class discussion or study questions

1. The social welfare system and the health care system overlap in areas of service as discussed in this chapter. Should they become one unified system? If so, what are the blocks to the two systems becoming unified?

2. What impact does the presence of a two-tier health care system have on meeting the health care needs of individuals and families?

3. In tracing the history of the development of health care and social welfare, how has social change and the system of resource distribution contributed to that development?

4. What is the impact of poverty ad racism-discrimination on meeting health care needs of individuals and families? Should the system be more open to considering cultural specific forms and methods of medicine and health care?

5. Are the federal government and the health care system adequately responding to the AIDS crisis? What more can be done? How does social work fit into the plan for response to this crisis ?

6. What roles should the federal government assume in the provision of health care services? What roles should state government assume? Which system of government should assume primary roles in the health care system?

7. What roles should the various health care professionals assume in the psycho-social care of individuals and their families? What roles should social workers assume? What should each of the professions contribute relative to on-going health planning within the system?

8. Are the health care related social welfare and social insurance programs (e.g., Medicaid, Medicare, maternal and child health programs) adequate to meet the health care needs of individuals and families who are unable to do so on their own? How will the proposed changes in how health care services are funded likely to affect the delivery of services?

9. Is the health care system making appropriate use of the services provided by hospitals, long-term care facilities and community settings? What changes should be made so that these components would be more responsive to health care needs of people?

10. Why hasn't the U.S. adopted a plan for national health insurance? What are the arguments for and against such a plan?

11. How is the HMO as a mechanism for delivery of health care services both preventative in design and a means for containing health care costs?

12. How has the medical model in the provision of health care services in the United States affected the roles and practice of social workers within the health care system?

13. If social workers are to take their rightful place among health care professionals, the profession must give attention to clarifying the roles of BSW and MSW practitioners in the health care field. How should this be done? What issues need to be taken into consideration?

E. Objective (multiple choice) examination questions. Choose the *best* response.

1. Social welfare and health care:

   a. are viewed by the public as the same delivery system.

   X b. have common concerns and themes and overlap in some areas of services designed to meet the health care needs of individuals and families.

   c. are totally different delivery systems focusing on different kinds of human need.

   d. are tightly controlled by different kinds of helping professionals.

2. Which of the following is a common concern of health care and social welfare:

   a. both systems are holistic (i.e., concerned with the whole person).

   b. both systems are concerned with environmental factors and prevention; both have used social reform and social control approaches to social problems.

   c. both systems have concern for the family, the relationship between illness and family functioning.

   X d. All of the above.

3. A contemporary public welfare mechanism for the coverage of health services for those who cannot afford to pay is:

X a. Medicaid.

   b. Medicare.

   c. social health and welfare programs.

   d. national health insurance.

4. The proposed changes in health care costs funding that is commonly referred to as "play or pay', is:

   a. the private market approach.

X b. employer-based approach.

   c. government-based approach

   d. the tax-based approach.

5. Part A of the Medicare program is designed to provide payment for:

   a. physician's fees.

X b. hospitalization and major medical costs.

   c. preventative health care services.

   d. only long-term care services.

6. Which of the following contributed to the introduction and involvement of social work as a profession in the health care system in the 1920s and 1930s?

   a. The development of a professional organization for social workers working in the system.

   b. Schools of social work offering specialized curriculum in medical social work.

   c. Establishment of the Veteran's Administration and development of social services in V.A. hospitals.

   d. Passage of the Sheppard-Towner Act creating maternal and child health centers.

   e. Passage of the Social Security Act of 1935

X f. all of the above.

7. Social services are required in the health care system in which of the following?

   a. Nursing homes where patients, care is funded by Medicare or Medicaid.

   b. Veterans Administration hospitals.

   c. Hospitals accredited by JCHA. d. HMOs and maternal and child health service agencies.

X e. all of the above.

8. The community setting component of the health care system

includes which of the following services?

   a. The hospital.

X b. private and group practices of physicians.

   c Nursing homes.

   d. Rehabilitation centers.

9 During the 1960s and 1970s social work roles in health care expanded due to which of the following:

   a. Social Security amendments of 1965 establishing Medicaid and Medicare.

   b. The Comprehensive Health Planning Act

   c. Requirement of JCHA that social services must be available to patients and families.

X d. all of the above.

10. The primary role of social workers in working with persons with AIDS is:

   a. obtaining funding for treatment.

   b. counteracting public ignorance about AIDS through community relations.

X c. empowering AIDS patients to give them decision-making power in policy decisions.

   d. assisting the families of AIDS victims.

11. Social workers employed in health care settings are:

   a. the primary health care providers.

   b. secondary health care providers.

X c. a part of a multi-disciplinary team made up of various health care professionals.

   d. tertiary health care providers.

12. The differentiation of roles between the MSW and BSW employed in health care settings is:

   a. well established.

X b. uncertain.

   c. non-existent.

   d. varies from setting to setting.

13. The role of the social worker in long-term health care facilities is a:

X a. generalist role, working with individuals, groups, families, the institution and the community .

   b. specialized role, related only to financial concerns of patients.

    c. primary health care provider.

    d. advocate, focusing on the changing of social policy.

14. A primary community-based health care agency that provides preventative services and has as a purpose to contain the high cost of medical care is:

    a. diagnostic related group care facility.

    b. out-patient community clinics.

X c. health maintenance organizations

    d. maternal-child health agency.

Chapter 10

Social welfare and mental health

An individual's mental health status is a factor that contributes to the inability of some individuals to meet their own basic needs and live satisfying lives. The field of practice within the social welfare system known as mental health services has developed to meet the needs of such persons struggling with their social functioning. This chapter helps students develop an understanding of what constitutes mental health, the development of mental health services from an historical perspective, the structure of the current mental health services delivery system, the role of social work in the delivery of mental health services and current concerns and issues for social workers who deliver mental health services. Case examples are provided to illustrate the services delivered to persons with mental health problems and the nature of social work practice in the mental health services delivery system. Also included in discussion of the mental health field of practice was consideration for two areas that might be considered emerging fields: developmental disabilities and drug and alcohol treatment.

A. Key points and issues

1. The concepts of mental illness and mental health are diffi-cult to define. Several definitions are presented in the text, each of which uses different perspectives and factors as the basis for the definition. Some definitions of these concepts incorporate the use of medical (psychiatric) diagnosis, (DSM-IV) while others incorporate social-environmental and cultural factors. A functional approach toward defining these concepts is taken in this chapter, using a service de-livery approach. Mental health services refers to services provided by mental health agencies, psychiatric hospitals, psychiatric units in general hospitals, community mental health centers and child guidance clinics. Services are pro-vided by these agencies to persons who have been diag-nosed as experiencing psychiatric disorders.

2. Other areas of service within the mental health services delivery system are also addressed. They are: treatment for alcohol and drug addiction and abuse, often provided by community mental health centers; and services for the developmentally disabled, historically considered part of the mental health field.

3. The historical development of mental health services is presented in the text. The key points to emphasize in the presentation of this material are:

a. With the emergence of the industrial society in the United States in the late 1800s, care for the mentally ill was provided within the emerging formal social welfare system under the provision of state poor laws and institutional systems. The emphasis at this time was on custodial care and not on treatment. In the 1800s, mental institutions, "insane asylums,,, were established to separate the mentally ill from the general populations of the poor law institutions. However, the focus of care remained custodial.

b. In the 1800s and early 1900s, reform efforts were made to change the system from a custodial to treatment oriented system. These were the reform movements led by Dorthea Dix in the 1840s and 1850s and the reform efforts headed by Clifford Beers in the early 1900s.

c. Beginning in the 1940s and continuing to the present time, several pieces of legislation have influenced and shaped the structure of mental health services. They are: The National Mental Health Act (1946), the Community Mental Health Centers Act (1963), The Comprehensive Health Planning and Public Health Service Amendments (1966) and the Mental Health Systems Act (1980).

d. Other events have also influenced the structure of mental health services. Important to consider are: the beginning of the use of psychotropic drugs in the 1950s, which made the management of the mentally ill much easier; the concept of the "therapeutic community,, within institutional settings; the emergence of community mental health centers in the 1960s and 1970s; the movement for deinstitutionalization; and most recently, the focus on severe and persistent mental illness and provision of services to those affected under the community support programs.

4. Services to the developmentally disabled have changed substantially over the years—from an institutional to community-based approach. Legislation such as P.L. 94-142,

the Education for All Handicapped Children Act and the advocacy efforts of the National Association of Retarded Citizens have brought about these changes.

5. The treatment of substance abuse (e.g., alcohol and drug addiction and abuse) are component services of a community mental health center. Therefore, the development of understandings about these national problems is important to understanding the range of mental health services.

6. Social work has had a significant history of involvement in the field of mental health services, beginning in the early 1900s and continuing through the present time. Social work is one of the primary professions and has had the most involvement in this field.

7. Social workers perform a variety of roles and functions within the mental health services delivery system. They are employed in psychiatric hospitals, psychiatric units of the general hospitals, community mental health centers and child guidance clinics. Social workers engage in providing clinical/therapeutic services, including individual, group and family therapy and indirect service activities such as community organization, supervision-teaching, planning and evaluation, administration and community consultation services. While many of these services are provided by MSW-level social workers, in recent years expanded roles have emerged for the BSW, particularly in areas of service designed for those who suffer from severe and persistent mental illness (e.g., community support programs, substance abuse and services for the developmentally disabled).

8. Enormous changes in the care of the mentally ill have occurred in the last two decades. There has been a change in emphasis from mental illness to mental health. With these changes have come several issues and concerns within the mental health field. These include: the impact of court decisions relative to the care and treatment of the mentally ill, funding concerns for mental health services including issues relative to public funding mechanisms, e.g., Medicaid, Medicare and private health insurance.

B. It is likely that students will have considerable interest in this field of practice. Instructors should be careful to point out that, although the knowledge and skills needed for practice within this field are largely clinical and require advanced training (MSW degree), there is a definite role for the BSW in the delivery of mental health services, particularly with the population who suffer from severe and persistent mental illness.

The student should develop the following.

1. An understanding of the definitions of mental illness, mental health and mental health services.

2. An understanding of the historical development of mental health services, with a particular emphasis on how this field of practice has undergone substantial changes over time.

3. A general understanding of social policies and legislation which have influenced and shaped the structure of the mental health services delivery system.

4. An understanding of how the use of psychotropic drugs, the development of the therapeutic community, the emergence of community mental health centers, deinstitutionalization and the recent focus on severe and persistent mental illness have influenced and shaped the provision of services in this field.

5. An understanding that services to the developmentally disabled and to persons experiencing problems with substance abuse are component services within the field of mental health services.

6. An understanding of the variety of roles and functions performed by social workers in the delivery of mental health services. Particular emphasis should be placed on the roles and functions of the BSW-level practitioner.

7. An understanding of the changes that have occurred in the care of the mentally ill and the issues of current concern within the field.

C. Suggested learning activities

1. The use of visual media on areas of service within this field.

2. The use of guest speakers or panels of practitioners to speak to the class on particular areas of service within the field. If possible a class field trip to a psychiatric hospital for a tour and explanation of services, would be most helpful in assisting students in their learning about this field of practice.

3. Using case examples or materials is always important in assisting students in their learning. To assist students in understanding the roles of a social worker (BSW) in a community support program that provides services to the chronic patient, divide the class into groups and have them read the case example

presented in this chapter. As a group, have them evaluate the intervention activities of the social worker in this case by discussing the following points:

   a. What did the social worker assess to be the client's needs in this situation?

   b. What plans did the social worker develop that would meet those needs?

   c. What community resources and other benefits did the social worker utilize as a part of the intervention plan?

   d. How did the social worker monitor and follow up on the plan for this client?

D. Class discussion or study questions

  1. Why are mental health services considered a field of practice within the social welfare system?

  2 Why are the concepts of mental illness and mental health difficult to define? How do you think these concepts should be determined? What are your definitions of these concepts?

  3. Should services for the developmentally disabled be included in the field of mental health? If not where should they be placed? Support your answer with reasons.

  4. Should substance abuse and addiction treatment services be included in the field of mental health? If so, why? If not, why?

  5. How has the care and treatment of the mentally ill changed from the 1800s to the present time? In what ways do you see earlier patterns of care still present in the mental health services delivery system?

  6. What social policy or legislative actions have brought about changes in the structure and delivery of mental health services? What impact have they had?

  7. How has the use of psychotropic drugs and the development of the "therapeutic community,, changed the nature of services provided to patients in psychiatric hospitals?

  8. Discuss the problems of deinstitutionalization. What can be done to overcome the problem? Are there some individuals who should remain in institutions?

  9. What services are provided by community mental health centers? Are these services always provided exclusively to persons experiencing problems with mental health?

10 . What services are provided to persons who suffer from severe and persistent mental illness by community support programs? What roles do social workers assume in the delivery of these services?

11. What are the major differences in the work done by MSWs and BSWs in the mental health field of practice?

12. Discuss the ramifications of the involvement of the courts in determining policies for the treatment of the mentally ill. Has this led to better service or negatively affected service provision? Support your thinking.

13. How can the rights of individuals and the protection of society be better insured relative to mental illness? Should society have the right to institutionalize persons who pose no threat to themselves or others? Support your thinking.

14. How can the care and treatment of the "underserved,, by the mental health services delivery system be effectively accomplished? What services are needed that are not now available? Should responsibility for serving this population be with the mental health service system, the social welfare system, or both?

E. Objective (multiple choice) examination questions. Choose the *best* response.

1. The concepts of mental illness and mental health are:

   a. easy to define.

X b. difficult to define because a multiplicity of factors that must be considered in defining them.

   c. one in the same, no distinction should be made between them.

   d. two separate and distinct concepts.

2. The relationship between social welfare and mental health services can best be described in which of the following ways?

   a. The social welfare system provides for the needs of persons in a poor state of mental health due to their lack of social and economic resources.

   b. The social welfare system attempts to meet the social and economic needs of persons so that a poor state of mental health can be prevented.

X c. Both of the above.

   d. There is no relationship. They are two separate and distinct delivery systems.

3. Officially, the definition of what is mental illness or who is mentally ill incorporates the use of:

X a. medical (psychiatric) diagnosis using the DSM III-R.

b. social-environmental factors.

c. cultural factors.

d. legal factors and processes.

4. Mental health services include:

a. institutional-hospital care.

b. services to the severe and persistently mental ill.

c. services to the developmentally disabled.

d. substance abuse services.

X e. all of the above.

5. Prior to the 1830s the care and treatment of the mentally ill was provided by:

a. state poor law institutions.

b. state "insane asylums.,,

X c. both of the above.

d. state psychiatric hospitals.

6. Changes in the care and treatment of the mentally ill in the 1900s received its major impetus from the work of:

a. Dorthea Dix.

b. Sigmund Freud.

X c. Clifford Beers.

d. Jane Addams.

7. The National Mental Health act of 1946 provided for:

a. research on the prevention and treatment of mental illness.

b. the training of mental health professionals.

c. the creation of the National Institute for Mental Health.

d. providing grants in aid to the states for programs in treating mental health disorders.

X e. all of the above.

8. The introduction and use of psychotropic drugs in the 1950s:

a. made the management of the mentally ill much easier.

b. reduced bizarre behavior and symptoms of illnesses resulting in better access of the patient to treatment.

c. allowed significant numbers of patients in psychiatric hospitals to be discharged.

X d. all of the above.

9 The legislation that provided funding for development of community mental health centers is:

a. National Mental Hygiene Act.

    b. Mental Health Study Act.

X c. Community Mental Health Centers Act.

    d. Action for Mental Health.

10. The current focus of the mental health services delivery system is on:

    a. the acutely mentally ill person.

X b. the severe and persistent mental illness.

    c. the marginally mentally ill person.

    d. the partially mentally ill person.

11. Assessment of the community mental health services delivery system tends to indicate that the system focuses on:

    a. service provision on verbal, middle class, non-psychotic patients who are not in danger of hospitalization.

    b. chronic patients have been neglected.

X c. both of the above.

    d. only those persons who have the ability to pay for services.

12. The legislation which brought about a change from institutional to community-based care for the developmentally disabled is:

X a. Education for All Handicapped Children Act (P.L. 94-142).

    b. National Developmentally Disabled Persons Act.

    c. National Mental Health and Mental Retardation Act.

    d. National Handicapped Persons Education Act.

13. Social workers in the mental health services delivery system assume which one of the following roles:

    a. clinical-direct therapy roles.

    b. indirect service roles (e.g., administration, planning, community organization).

X c. both of the above

    d. Secondary roles not assumed by other mental health professionals.

14. Which of the following groups of persons are considered to be the "underserved,, as far as mental health services are concerned:

    a. the poor.

    b. the aged.

    c. the severely and persistently mental ill.

    d. the developmentally disabled.

X e. all of the above.

15. In recent years the primary role of the BSW level practitioner in working in community mental health service delivery systems has been in:

   a. community psychiatric hospitals

X b. community support programs (case management role with chronically mentally ill).

   c. providing therapeutic counseling in community mental health centers

   d. providing out-patient, private practice counseling and services.

Chapter 11

Social work and corrections

This chapter introduces students to the field of juvenile and adult corrections, which often are not considered a part of the U.S. social welfare system. The authors believe that juvenile and adult corrections should be considered a field of practice within social welfare. Social welfare and corrections are not two clearly separate systems of response to human need. Although the social welfare system focuses on providing for broader human needs, both systems have as their overall concern the improvement of human social functioning. The social work profession bridges the gap between the two systems. Social workers are significantly involved in both systems. To assist the student in understanding the total structure and scope of social welfare, this chapter on the field of corrections is included.

A. Key points and issues

1. Social work and corrections have experienced difficulties in working together. Corrections personnel and social workers, ways of functioning are based on conflicting values. These value conflicts are described in the text.

2. The criminal justice system is comprised of three parts: law enforcement, the judicial system and the correctional system. This chapter focuses on corrections. Corrections, in a broad sense, is the part of the system that deals with the causes of crime and delinquency and implements social control measures that treat and rehabilitate offenders. Corrections can also be thought of as a professional service that applies a criminology knowledge base to the control and rehabilitation of the criminal offender.

3. The juvenile corrections system today consists of institutional services and community-based services. Institutional services are those in which the juvenile is placed in a closed setting. Community-based services are those that exist in an open community setting. There are formal and informal institutional services as well as formal and informal community-based services. Formal services are those which are mandated by law

or provided by a governmental unit (e.g., local and state). Informal services are those made available to juvenile offenders through private voluntary social service agencies. Examples of these areas of service are provided in the text.

4. The adult corrections system is similar in structure to the juvenile system. There are institutional, community-based, formal and informal service delivery arrangements within the system.

5. The juvenile justice system began in the United States with the emergence of the juvenile court in the late 1870s. The juvenile court was founded on a principle of Roman common law, *parens patriae,* which means the power of the state to act in behalf of a child as a wise parent would do. The juvenile court is not a criminal court. Non-adversary legal procedures are used and the best interests of the juvenile are taken into consideration. The aim of the court is to educate, treat and rehabilitate the juvenile offender. Prior to the formation of the juvenile court, a child was treated no differently than the adult offender. Recently a "get tough" philosophy has emerged and may alter the traditional mission of juvenile courts.

6. Although the juvenile court was founded on the above philosophies, what would be in the best interests of the child was not always taken fully into consideration. Many juvenile courts became quite paternalistic and punitive, often violating the constitutional and legal rights of parents and children. In 1967 the United States Supreme Court, in the case of *Gault v. Arizona,* ruled that juvenile court procedures were in violation of due process of law rights. This ruling brought forth changes in juvenile court procedures and laws which now afford juveniles the right to due process of law.

7. Juvenile offenders come under the jurisdiction of the juvenile court in two primary ways. One, if the child commits an offense which violates the law (e.g., burglary to murder, misdemeanors to felonies), they are charged as a delinquent child. Second, juvenile courts can also assume jurisdiction over children who commit offenses associated with their status (e.g., running away, out of control of parents). These children are labeled as status offenders. There has been considerable effort on behalf of the juvenile court in recent years to divert status offenders away from the formal system.

The causes of juvenile delinquency are complex. Research in the past attempted to explain delinquent behavior from biological, psychological and sociological theoretical orientations. More recently, peer influence and older theories such as social control theory and strain theory have been used to explain group delinquency, particularly the emergence of juvenile gangs, which has become a significant problem Other research suggests that juvenile delinquency is the beginning stage of causes of criminality. While problems within the delinquent's family system has been seen as closely associated with delinquency, recent research has concluded a weaker relationship between family system problems and delinquency.

9. Treatment methods and approaches for both juvenile delinquents and status offenders vary, depending on the child's individual situation. The treatment of delinquents has become more complicated recently due to the number of violent crimes committed by juveniles. A new area of treatment has also emerged, that is treatment of adolescent sex offenders. Juvenile courts have discretionary power in rendering decisions concerning the treatment of both categories of these children. Examples of possible treatment approaches for both are discussed in the text.

10. Social workers assume a variety of roles within both the formal and informal juvenile corrections system. They may work within the formal system as a probation officer, perform administrative roles, and work in juvenile corrections institutions. Social workers perform a variety of roles in the informal juvenile corrections system, mostly in community-based programs and agencies which serve the juvenile offender. Examples are provided in the text.

11. The adult corrections system focuses on understanding crime, treating and rehabilitating the offender, and the prevention of crime. A number of theories have evolved historically as to the causes of crime. Currently, the multiple causation theory, which combines biological, social, psychological, economic and environmental factors, is widely accepted.

12. Societal responses to the adult criminal offender have fluctuated between being punishment oriented or rehabilitation oriented. Current adult corrections policy tends to be more punishment oriented, dominated by the idea of "just deserts." This philosophy is reflected by the fact that more dollars are

being spent in the building of prisons than ever before. The renewed practice of capital punishment is also reflective of this view. This trend in policy appears to be gaining strength, prompted by new views that are discussed in the chapter.

13. Although much reform has occurred in the adult prison system over the years, some problems continue to exist. The most pressing of these today is overcrowding, which has led to new or expanded prisons. There has also been movement toward the privatization of corrections, which is discussed in the chapter.

14. Community-based adult correctional services are designed to provide treatment and rehabilitative measure in the community as an alternative to institutionalization. Probation and parole services include: work and educational release, restitution, halfway houses, drug treatment programs, mental health services, and other social, health and recreational services.

15. The adult criminal population is diverse; each individual has his/her own unique needs. There are differences in the way that the correctional system deals with individuals. Diverse characteristics such as race, socio-economic status, and gender all play a significant part in how the system deals with offender.

16. The diverseness of adult offenders is evident when considering special needs offenders (e.g., mentally ill, developmentally disabled, sex offenders, aged offenders, HIV-infected offenders and dangerous offenders). The current corrections system is ill-equipped to deal with these offenders, but must, in the future, begin to address their needs.

17. Social workers have performed a variety of roles, both within community-based adult corrections services and in some correctional institutions. Social workers have filled positions as probation and parole officers. In recent years social workers have become employed in police departments, performing crisis intervention roles and working in domestic violence intervention programs. More recently both undergraduate and graduate social work programs have begun to offer course work and field training for students interested in correctional social work.

B. Students have become quite interested in this field of practice in recent years. It is important that students in an introductory course be introduced to this field of practice so that it can be considered as a career option.

The student should develop the following.

1. An understanding of the concept of corrections and the role of correctional services in the overall framework of the criminal justice system. An ability to identify the three components of the criminal justice system.

2. An understanding of the juvenile corrections system, both the formal and informal, the community-based and institutional parts of the system.

3. An understanding of the structure of the juvenile court, its processes and missions and how reform has taken place in its legal processes, with particular focus on due process of law.

4. An understanding of how children come under the jurisdiction of the juvenile court, the differences between the labels of delinquent and status offender, and the current focus on diversion of the status offender away from the formal system.

5. An understanding of the treatment approaches and methods for juvenile delinquents and status offenders .

6. An understanding of the roles performed by social workers within the formal-informal, community-based and institutional components of the juvenile corrections system.

7. An understanding of the structure and missions of the adult corrections system and theories of causation of adult crime.

8. An understanding that societal responses to the criminal offender through the adult corrections system have been influenced at various times by the opposing philosophies of punishment versus rehabilitation and treatment. Students should become aware of the philosophies of current corrections policy.

9. An understanding of the adult corrections system and its component parts of the community-based services and institutional services and an awareness of the impact of social policy issues, legislation and legal decisions on the structure and functioning of the system.

10. An understanding of the community-based adult correctional services system.

11. An understanding of and sensitivity to human diversity issues as they affect the way in which adult offenders are treated by the system.

12. An understanding of the issues associated with special needs offenders and how the system needs to move in the direction of responding adequately to their needs.

13. An understanding of the various roles performed by social workers in the adult corrections system.

C. The instructor can use several types of learning activities to teach the content of this chapter and enrich students' understanding of this field of practice. The use of guest speakers from the corrections field to speak on corrections topics would be useful. If possible, a tour of a correctional facility or institution would be a real "eye opener', for the students and would help them see first-hand the realities faced by offenders who are incarcerated. One should use visual media, if available. One suggested classroom learning activity would be to divide the students into groups and have them discuss or debate correctional issues such as punishment (the "just deserts,, model of corrections) versus treatment and rehabilitation, capital punishment, community-based versus institutional-based corrections, or how to deal with special needs offenders.

D. Class discussion or study questions

1. What is the basis for value conflicts that exist between social workers and other corrections professionals? What can be done to resolve this conflict?

2. Define the term corrections. Should correctional services be construed as only those services provided within the formal system? Should it be viewed more broadly to include the services provided by the entire social welfare system?

3. How does the structure and mission of the juvenile corrections system differ from that of the adult corrections system?

4. What factors account for the fact that juvenile crime is on the rise, especially violent crime?

5. What are the arguments for and against diversion of the status offender from the jurisdiction of the juvenile court? Why do some of these offenders ,'fall through the cracks', of the system and not receive adequate services?

6. Has society, through the juvenile court, become tougher on the offender than is evident in the current system?

7. Should society become more concerned with the causes, treatment, and prevention of crime, rather than developing correctional services which focus on punishment of the offender?

8. Do prisons succeed in acting as a deterrent to the incidence of crime? What factors suggest that it does not? What are the changes that private corrections will be any more effective than publicly administered facilities?

9. What is a reasonable way to deal with violent behavior within the penal institution? Would placing more emphasis on treatment and rehabilitation of the offender be helpful in this effort?

10. Should more emphasis be placed on community based correctional services for adults? Why do you think society has put more of its resources into the construction of prisons than in the development of community-based services?

11. Should special needs offenders receive deferential treatment within the system? Is the system responsible for meeting these offenders, needs as opposed to responsibility for punishing the offenders and protecting society from them?

E. Objective (multiple choice) examination questions. Choose the *best* response.

1. Social work values and the values of other corrections personnel are often:

   a. compatible with each other.

X b. in conflict with each other.

   c. neither compatible or in conflict with each other.

   d. different in some instances, the same in other instances.

2. The term corrections means;

   a. to study, understand and treat the causes of crime and to deal with its prevention.

   b. to provide measures of social control on those who commit criminal acts.

X c. both of the above.

   d. to punish the offender with the goal of correcting his/her behaviors.

3. The juvenile corrections system is comprised of which of the following?

   a. Formal institutional settings

   b. informal institutional settings

   c. formal community-based services

   d. informal community-based services

X e. all of the above

4. The concept of Roman common law which formed the basis for the development of the juvenile court in the 1800s and gave it power to act in behalf of children is:

   a. Judeo-Christian ethic.

X b. Parens Patriae.

   c. due process of law.

   d. Caveat Emptor.

5. The *Gault v. Arizona* Supreme Court decision provided which of the following concerning juvenile court procedure?
   a. created an adversary proceeding
   b. expanded the powers of the court
   X c. established due process of law rights for juveniles
   d. revoked due process of law rights for juveniles

6. The treatment of juveniles who are adjudicated as delinquent has become more complicated recently because of:
   a. resources and funds to support treatment.
   b. a lack of support in the courts.
   c. a policy shift away from treatment.
   d. an increase of violent crimes committed by juveniles.
   X e. all of the above.

7. Diversion of status offenders away from the jurisdiction of the court refers to:
   X a. the notion that they can be better served by community child welfare and social service agencies.
   b. institutionalization of the status offender.
   c. de-institutionalization of the status offender.
   d. the court would rather not serve such children.

8. A status offender is:
   a. a child who has committed an act that violates law (e.g., burglary).
   X b. a child who commits acts associated with their status as a juvenile (e.g., running away form home).
   c. a child with special needs (e.g., a developmental disability).
   d. a child who has committed only minor crimes (e.g., misdemeanors).

9. Social workers in the juvenile corrections system perform which of the following roles?
   a. probation officer
   b. administrative role
   c. work in a corrections institution
   d. work in community based agencies providing services to juvenile offenders
   X e. all of the above

10. The theory of causation of crime which combines a number of factors in attempting to explain why crime occurs is:

    a. the religious theory of crime.

    b. the constitution school of crime.

X c. the multiple causation theory of crime.

    d. the combined theory of crime.

11. The privatization of corrections refers to:

    a. the use of private funds to build prisons.

X b. the use of private not-for-profit or for-profit facilities to incarcerate offenders.

    c. allowing more privacy to inmates incarcerated in penal institutions.

    d. the use of privately funded, publicly-managed facilities.

12. Which of the following services is a part of the adult community based corrections system?

    a. law enforcement

X b. work educational release

    c. prisons and jails

    d. psychiatric correctional facilities

13. In the U.S. today, women's correctional facilities are:

X a. more progressive than men's facilities.

    b. less progressive than men's facilities.

    c. less secure, with less stringent discipline than men's facilities.

    d. more secure, with more stringent discipline than men's facilities.

14. Human diversity among adult offenders is especially evident when considering how the system deals with:

    a. race.

    b. socioeconomic status.

    c. gender.

X d. special needs offenders.

15. Which of the following is a role performed by social workers in the adult corrections system?

    a. probation/parole officer

    b. prison social worker

    c. police social worker

X d. all of the above

Chapter 12

Gerontological social work

This chapter introduces the student to social work with the aged or gerontological social work. This field of practice is a fairly recent addition to the social welfare system. Although the profession of social work has always had concern for the needs of older persons in society and formal social welfare arrangements have been used throughout time to meet the needs of the aged, this field of practice has emerged over the last twenty-five years. As the life span lengthened and the number of older persons increased, the need for special attention to this population group also has grown. Thus, it is appropriate that a special field of practice has developed that focuses on the problems associated with aging and aged persons. The student will be able to identify the aged in society, problem/conditions that cause needs in living for this group, special concerns or problem areas faced by the aged, social welfare arrangements provided to meet the needs of these persons, social policy that affects the delivery of services to aged persons, and the involvement of and the roles of social workers in the delivery of services to this population.

A. Key points presented in this chapter.

1. Interest in the needs and concerns of the aged began in the mid-1940s with the formation of the Gerontological Society. Interest intensified in the 1960s as a result of the first White House Conference on Aging, which formed the basis for important legislation such as the Older Americans Act and the Medicare/Medicaid amendments to the Social Security Act.

2. The aged in U.S. society is a diverse group, made up of individuals with varying characteristics. Demographic data are provided in the text relative to various characteristics of the aged (e.g., age, race, gender, developmental status, social, economic and geographic). Officially, society considers individuals age 65 and older to be the aged.

3. Contemporary U.S. society displays considerable prejudice against the aged—referred to as "ageism." Attitudes toward older persons and the aging process are generally negative. Society values youth, physical fitness and productivity.

4 Not all aged persons are in need of attention from the social welfare system. Some are able to supply their own needs from their own resources or from their immediate personal network. But a significant number are at risk. Factors that put older people at rise are insufficient income, living alone with no family nearby, poor health, negative attitudes about aging, and being over 75 years old. When these risk factors impair the individual's capacity to function, social welfare and social service resources are needed.

5. The social welfare arrangements identified earlier in the text have all come into use with respect to meeting the needs of aged persons throughout history. Of particular significance are the arrangements of public welfare, including Medicaid, social insurance for the aged, Medicare, and social service provision.

6. Current concerns and issues in providing for the needs of the aged are directly related to each of the conditions which give rise to human needs (social change, poverty, lack of resources, and discrimination.) The needs, concerns, and problems faced by the aged in contemporary U.S. society fall into each of these problem/condition areas.

7. There are many questions to be answered and many issues to be addressed if the U.S. social welfare system is to meet the needs of all aged persons. Of particular concern in recent years is the issue of long-term care for the frail elderly. This is the fastest growing population in the United States. A large proportion of these persons are not institutionalized (e.g., nursing homes). The social welfare system has developed a number of supportive services (e.g., home-delivered meals, home health care, adult day care, etc.) in the community to address the needs of such persons. For those in need of services, because they cannot remain in their own homes, emphasis is being placed on short-term nursing facility placements or other alternatives to nursing home care, such as assisted living facilities, etc.

8. Social workers work with the aged in the community and in institutions. Social workers perform a wide variety of roles. Some of the more important are: broker, providing older persons and their families with information on services which may

be available, and as a case manager coordinating a wide variety services. Social workers must also work with the family caregivers to support the care they provide to their aged parent or relatives. Social workers use a number of practice approaches with older persons. Included are crisis intervention, group work, and planning and development of community services. Empowerment-oriented practice with this population has recently become a useful approach to service delivery. Some social workers also carry administrative responsibilities in agencies which serve the aged.

B Gerontological social work has grown in popularity with students in recent years, as the field itself has developed. Students will likely be interested in this field and should be encouraged to consider it as a possible career choice.

Students should develop the following.

1. The field of gerontological social work is fairly recent in origin, developing within the last twenty-five years. Students should develop understandings about the historical events which have brought about its development.

2. Understanding the biological, psychological, and social factors that affect the aging population.

3. The aged are a diverse group, made up of persons with various characteristics. Students need to gain sensitivity to and understandings about the diverse characteristics and human development process associated with this special population.

4. An understanding of and sensitivity to the societal attitudes and behaviors which bring forth prejudice and discrimination toward the aged.

5. An understanding of the factors which place older persons at risk for dysfunction and prevent them from living a satisfying life.

6. An understanding of social welfare/social services policies programs and services which assist aged persons in U.S. society.

7. An understanding of the impact of the social conditions of poverty, lack of resources and discrimination on the functioning and well-being of aged persons

8. An understanding of the needs of aged persons, such as economic, roles in society and health care. The student should also develop an understanding of the broad service provision areas which focus on the meeting of these needs.

9. An understanding of the various roles performed by social workers in both community and institutional settings that provide services to aged persons.

C. Several learning activities could be utilized in assisting student learning about this field of practice. You may find it useful to utilize the expertise of community practitioners from institutional settings such as a nursing home, community settings such as day service programs for the aged, or senior citizens centers. They can speak to students on social work practice issues. It would also be useful to have groups of students visit a community provider of services (e.g., nursing home, senior center, adult day care center, area agency on aging) to learn first-hand the services provided and the roles performed by social workers. Video media dealing with service provision to the aged would also be useful in enriching the students, learning about this field. Case materials, such as presented in this chapter, and classroom learning activities, utilizing the discussion questions from the text or this manual, could be used to assist the students in critically analyzing the issues and problems that confront aged persons and social work's response to them.

Suggested learning activities

1. To assist the students in developing understandings about the needs of aging persons and in analyzing how current social welfare/social service delivery arrangements respond to their needs, assign the students to four discussion groups and have them review Chart I and the social welfare/social service arrangements presented and discussed in the text. Assign each of the groups one of the broad service delivery areas from Chart I: (1) preventative care, (2) socialization, (3) supportive and protective care, and (4) institutional care. Have each group analyze how the current social welfare/social service arrangements respond to the need areas of economic, attitudinal, rolelessness and health care for their broad service delivery area. Encourage each group to consider how well the arrangements meet needs and critically analyze and identify the gaps in meeting needs for their area. Have each group report their discussion and findings orally to the entire class.

2 To assist students in understanding what it is like to be an aged person in today's society, have the students interview an aged persons (e.g., grandparent or other relative, friend of the family, etc.). In the interview, have the students focus on the following:

    a. How does the person view the aging experience.

    b. What problems or concerns do they have in living as an aged person?

    c. What do they see as resources or support for coping with the aging process?

Require students to provide a brief written report on their interview, using chapter material as a resource to support their findings, or how their findings conflict with the material found in the text.

3. Divide the class into groups and provide each a case example (i.e., the example in the text). Have each group analyze the role of the social worker in working with the identified client in the case example by discussing the following issues and questions.

    a. What are the needs in the case situation?

    b. What were the social work practice strategies used by the social worker in intervening with the case situation?

    c. What social welfare/social service delivery arrangements were utilized in the case situation?

    d. What impact did the social workers intervention and use of social welfare/social service resources have on the outcome of the case situation?

D. Class study or discussion questions

1. What factors or events led to the emergence of gerontological social work as a field of practice? Should it be a separate field? Why do you think this?

2 What impact did the first White House Conference on Aging have on the development of important legislation authorizing service provision to the aged? What legislation did this?

3. What is meant by the statement: The aged are a diverse group? What accounts for diversity among this group? What diverse factors, including demographic and developmental factors, need to be considered when analyzing their need?

4. Why do so many people see aging or the aged stage of life as negative? How can attitudes be changed relative to this?

5. What is "ageism?,, Where does it occur? What effects does it have on the aged population relative to their social functioning?

6. What social/problem factors place the aged at risk? Do all aged persons manage these risk factors well? When and under what circumstances do the aged become in need of social welfare/ social service resources as a result of the risk factors?

7. What should be the role of the family in meeting the needs of aged persons? How can the service delivery system more support the care provided by family caregivers?

8. How do the arrangements of public welfare, social insurance, and social services respond to the needs of the aged in contemporary U.S. society? What individual programs are available?

9. Discuss the social changes which have taken place in the latter half of the current century which have had an impact on the aged. How have those who are now aged had to make changes in their way of life?

10. How has the phenomenon of retirement affected the aged? Should persons age 65 and older retire? Should older persons be allowed to work as long as they wish?

11. How and in what specific ways are the aged significantly affected by poverty?

12 What are the needs of the frail elderly for long-term community care? What must the social welfare system do to insure that these needs are met?

13. What are the differences between nursing homes and assisted living facilities?

14. How should need be determined for aged persons? Do you agree with the framework suggested in Chart I of the text? What other factors should be taken into consideration?

15 What roles are performed by social workers in institutional settings? In community settings? What practice strategies are utilized in service provision to aged persons?

E. Objective (multiple choice) examination questions.

1. Which one of the following organizations began to identify the needs and concerns of aged persons that formed the basis for important legislation affecting aged persons?
   a. Gerontological Society
   b. National Council on Aging
   X c. White House Conferences on Aging
   d. American Association of Retired Persons.

2. According to the text, a most important developmental task for aged persons is:

X a. maintenance of a positive self-concept.
 b. developing the capacity to cope with declining physical capacities.
 c. developing the capacity to deal with the prospect of death.
 d. developing the capacity to deal with limited income.

3. Increased emphasis on social welfare/social service delivery to aged persons in recent years has come as a result of:

 a. increased numbers of aged persons.
 b. helping professions becoming concerned with their needs.
 c. aged have acquired political influence.
X d. all of the above.

4. "Ageism,, involves:

 a. discrimination in the workplace against the aged.
 b. discrimination by the media.
 c. discrimination on the basis of stereotypes, e.g., aged are incompetent.
X d. all of the above.

5. The program of income maintenance designed to provide for the economic security of poor aged persons is:

 a. aid to families with dependent aged persons.
 b. old age survivors insurance (Social Security).
X c. Supplemental Security Income (SSI).
 d. aid to the elderly.

6. The most crucial current issue of concern for the frail elderly is their need for:

X a. long-term care.
 b. economic assistance.
 c. health care.
 d. protection from potential harm.

7. The primary funding for social services for the aged today is provided by which one of the following?

X a. Older Americans Act
 b. Title XX of the Social Security Act
 c. Old Age Assistance Act
 d. Elderly Americans Act

8. Social change in this century has affected the aged in which of the following ways:

    a. increased their numbers, fastest growing segment of the population.

    b. fostered their capacity to live longer increasing need for health care services .

    c. reduced family capacity to care for its older members.

X d. all of the above.

9. Which of the following factors put older people at risk?

    a. income problems

    b. living alone with no family nearby

    c. poor health

    d. negative attitudes about aging

    e. being over 75 years of age

X f. all of the above

10. A new resource for aged persons who need assistance with activities of daily living is:

    a. assisted home care.

    b. daily living activity centers

    c. ADL foster care

X d. assisted living facilities

11. Some elderly persons need a variety of services; therefore, coordination of resources by one worker is most effective. This function is referred to as:

    a. brokerage.

    b. advocacy.

    c. coordination.

X d. case management.

12. Social workers assume which of the following roles in work with aged persons?

    a. health/mental health roles

    b. financial support roles

    e. educational activities role

    d. nursing home social work role

X e. all of the above

Chapter 13

Organizing fields of practice by system type: groups, communities and families

The text, up to this point, has discussed fields of practice that relate to specific social problem/condition areas. However, not all social work practice is concerned with specific problem areas. This chapter focuses on fields of practice that are closely tied to methods of social work practice that deal with specific social systems, groups, communities and families.

Students will understand how these methods of social work practice have been used historically and are being used currently in the delivery of social services to various population groups and in bringing about change in the problem/conditions that interfere with their social functioning.

A. Key points and issues

1. Group services, community practice and family services are fields of social work practice that focus on a system type as their organizing theme.

2. The field of group services is usually limited to those services provided by agencies which identify themselves as group service agencies.

3. Group services and the group work method of social work practice share the same historical development, beginning with the settlement house movement and the use of group services by the youth-serving agencies.

4. As the group services field of practice began to mature, there was a need for conceptualization and education for the field. From the 1920s through the 1940s, schools of social work began to develop specializations or courses in group work. The formation of the American Association of Group Workers in 1976 clearly established this method of social work practice as part of the social welfare system.

5. During the early days of group services, several concerns emerged. The profession seemed divided about what the relationship should be between group work and group therapy. The debate revolved around whether group work should focus on the use of the group process to bring about change for the benefit of the group or should be a vehicle for treatment individuals (group therapy). This question has never been totally answered or resolved. The use of groups continued in service provided by traditional group service agencies and groups also began to use therapeutic processes, particularly in the psychiatric treatment of individuals.

6. The zenith of group service occurred during the 1940s and 50s, inspired by a growing body of knowledge and the development of a literature base in group work. During the 1960s social group work and the group field of practice declined in importance. Social workers with a group work backgrounds moved away from practice in traditional group service agencies to practice in other fields, particularly those with a social problem orientation which utilized group therapy services.

7. In the early 1970s, social work education began to develop the generalist practice method. This abolished the old group work begun in many schools of social work. Group work was supposed to become an integral part of the new generalist method taught at the undergraduate level, but integration has been sporadic and only partially achieved.

8. Currently, the major thrusts of the group field of practice, prevention, socialization and volunteerism, have given way to professionalism, therapy and problem-oriented practice activities. However, with contemporary concerns with the use of volunteers and self-help groups and the availability of the professional BSW social worker, there is a place for group services in the social welfare system. Current social problems (e.g., homelessness and drug abuse) could be partially addressed by the field of group services. The field could also serve as a focal point for the use of the rich resource of volunteers.

9. Community practice has always been considered a method of social work practice as well as a field of practice within the social welfare system. The major functions of a community organization agency are coordination, planning, funding and monitoring of services provided within the social welfare system, as well as community change and community building.

10. The roots of the historical development of community practice were within the private philanthropic charity movement (COS'S) and in the social action activities of the settlement houses. As the federal government became more involved in social welfare, new opportunities for community organizations emerged. There was an increased need for planning and coordination of services, and community organization practice became part of many government agencies. In the 1950s, community organization moved to a planning approach to the provision of social welfare services, gradually giving way to a social action approach in the 1960s.

Several important pieces of legislation moved the field in this direction. Most noteworthy was the Economic Opportunity Act of 1964 (War on Poverty). The legislation called for workers with education and skill in community organizations. From the 1970s to present, cuts in federal expenditures for social welfare and other means of funding social programs have changed the skills needed by community practitioners from planning skills to administrative and evaluation skills, as well as clinical skills. This has had an impact on the education and training of social workers in this field of practice.

11. Social workers in this field have always been considered specialists. Community practice as a method of social work practice was largely developed in graduate education and continued to develop there through the 1960s. With the emergence of the generalist practice focus in the 1970s, undergraduate education began to include some community practice theory and skill in its programs. However, this field largely remains a specialized one for social workers educated at the graduate level and has been absorbed into the division in graduate training known as macro practice which focuses on community planning, administration and social program evaluation.

12. Service to families is an important component of many social problem-oriented fields of practice (e.g., child welfare, health care, and mental health). However, a services to families field sees the family as a major concern for service. Some agencies within this field to healthy functioning. The focus is on the family as a social system regardless of what social problems may be involved.

13. Social and economic changes in the current century have resulted in enormous challenges for the family in contemporary society. The personal and social skills of some families to adjust and cope with demands in living have placed stresses on them and threatened their stability.

14. Changes have occurred in the current century in family structure and in what constitutes the definition of family. Prior to the turn of the century, the predominant family form was the extended family system. In contemporary society, the predominant family form is the nuclear family. Since 1970, several alternative family forms have emerged (e.g., single-parent family, step-family, childless family).

15. The welfare/social service delivery system does respond to families that experience problems. However, these responses have been designed mostly to assist individuals, rather than strengthen the family as a social unit. This is due to the absence of a national family social policy.

16. The tightening of income maintenance regulations in contemporary society has caused problems with economic security for some families. Poverty and homelessness are significant problems for some families. Adequate income is essential to successful family functioning. When the family lacks adequate income supports, its ability to perform other expected roles and functions is lessened, leading to tension, conflict and possible family dysfunction.

17. Income from employment is the most socially acceptable means for families to meet the basic living needs. Unemployment undermines the economic well-being of the family. For families who struggle with economic security, income maintenance programs are their primary source of assistance. Income maintenance programs such as AFDC, food stamps, Medicaid, and SSI are available to assist such families. Despite the availability of these programs, many families continue to struggle with economic security. Serious questions were raised by the WHCF as to whether society can expect troubled families to maintain their independence and self-sufficiency without adequate societal support mechanisms.

18. Two family relationship problems are addressed in the chapter. They are divorce and family violence. These problems by no means reflect all of the relationship problems experienced by families, but are the ones which have received considerable

attention from professionals concerned about the maintenance of the family as the primary social unit.

19. Social work has always had a central concern for working with troubled families and has used a variety of theoretical approaches and models in work with them. Social work practice in the family services field should focus on environmental concerns as they affect family functioning, working with communities, social action to influence social policy and working with individuals and groups in behalf of families.

B. It is important that students understand that fields of social work practice are organized by system type as well as by social problem/ condition areas or population groups. This assists students in further conceptualizing the profession and its goals, missions and purposes and acts to "professionally socialize students,,, of particular importance for the undergraduate student.

The students should develop the following.

1. An understanding that social work practice fields can focus on a system type as their organizing theme .

2. An understanding that the group field of practice and group work as a method of practice can be used to address a variety of social problems and serve as a vehicle for the provision of social welfare services.

3. An understanding of the major functions of community practices discussed in the text and of the roles of community practitioners in the provision of social welfare services.

4. An awareness that work with communities and community practice strategies is an important piece of the generalist approach to practice.

5. An understanding that the field of family services is an important component of problem-oriented fields of practice and should focus on the family as a social system.

6. An understanding that social and economic changes have had an impact on the family in numerous ways and have resulted in some families experiencing difficulties in carrying out their expected roles and functions in contemporary society.

7. An understanding that the responses made by the social welfare/social service delivery systems to assist troubled families are somewhat fragmented, due to the absence of a national social policy which has as its mission to strengthen and preserve the family.

8. Changes in income maintenance policy have caused problems with economic security for families. Students should gain new insights into the problems of poverty and homelessness for families .

9. A basic understanding of income maintenance programs and how they assist families who struggle with adequate income supports.

10 An understanding of the family-centered problems of divorce and family violence and the responses made via social service delivery with these problems.

11. An understanding of the social welfare delivery system for troubled families and the role of social workers in the delivery of such services.

C. A variety of learning activities can be used to assist students in understanding these system type fields of practice.

Suggested learning activities

For The Group Services Field of Practice

1. Have a panel of group service practitioners discuss how groups are used to deliver various types of services. Select practitioners from a variety of group service agencies (e.g., youth service, therapeutic, etc.).

2. Have the students attend an open meeting of AA or some other type of self-help group. Have them record their observations of the process by which help is given and received by the group members Have students find out how referrals are made to these types of groups or how people get linked to their services.

3. If possible, have the students or groups of students observe (perhaps through a one-way mirror) a group therapy session. A word of caution here: Be sure to remind students of the confidential nature of what they will be observing and how confidentiality is expected of students in professional training.

4. Have the students visit a local volunteerism agency to learn which services in the community are provided by groups of volunteers. Do the services seem to be fulfilling a need? Are there problems in the use of volunteers to deliver the services?

For the Community Practice Field of Practice

1 Have the students visit a local United Way or similar agency to learn how funds are raised and distributed for various types of services in the community. Have students ascertain the roles of staff employed in the agency.

2 If possible, have the students attend a civil rights or community social action group meeting to learn about issues in the community. Require students to record what methods are being proposed by the group to deal with their concerns and make changes. Following the visit, engage the students in a discussion about their observations.

3. Select a social problem and have the students look up in a community service directory or telephone directory the services available in the community to deal with the selected problem. If the information in the directories is not clear, encourage the students to ask for additional information. Engage the students in discussion about what gaps exist in services for the problem? How could a community practitioner work with the community to fill in the gaps?

4. Have groups of students contact a local social service agency in your community to ascertain how it is evaluated and by whom. Have each group report to the class, answering the following questions. Does the evaluation process seem to deal with pertinent issues? Are there provisions in the evaluation process for consumer evaluation of services provided?

For the Family Services Field of Practice

1. Invite practitioners to speak on various aspects of services to families (e.g., a family therapist, a social worker working in a domestic violence program, shelter for the homeless or drug treatment agency).

2. Visual materials, such as video cassettes or films, on particular aspects of family services would contribute to student learning.

3. The students understanding of this field will be greatly enhanced by the use of classroom learning activities based on case examples or materials that require student "hands on,' experience.

D. Class discussion or study questions

1. What contributions have been made by the group services field of practice to the delivery of social services? What contributions have been made to the generalist approach to social work practice.

2. How has the group services field of practice changed over the years? What factors account for its decline? Is it still a valid field of practice within the social welfare system? Support your answer.

3. How can volunteer groups or the use of self-help groups be more effectively utilized to deliver social welfare services? Support your answer by giving examples.

4. What are the major functions of community organization as a field of practice? Have these changed over the years?

5. Is community organization a specialized field of practice within social welfare? What special knowledge do social workers as community organizers need to have? What knowledge of community organization does the generalist need to have?

6. With the cutbacks in funding for social welfare services, has the role of the community organizer changed? Has the change of role been positive or negative? Should community organizers be doing more to promote quantity and quality of services to effectively meet existing human need? Support your answer.

7. Social and economic changes have brought about changes in family structure, roles and functions. What changes with regard to the above have occurred? How have these changes caused instability in some families?

8. What new variant family forms have emerged since the turn of the century? How has their emergence given rise to new concerns and problem conditions relative to the meeting of family needs.

9. Social welfare responses to the family have been structured to meet the needs and assist individuals within families rather than assist the family as a unit. How has the absence of unified national policy on families contributed to this?

10. Poverty and homelessness are significant problems for some families. What does the lack of adequate income supports do to a family's ability to function? How does this lead to possible family dysfunction?

11. What are the causes of family violence in contemporary society? What responses have been made by the social services delivery system and the judicial system to deal with this problem/condition?

12. What recommendations did the White House Conference on Families make about changes in social policy that would strengthen and preserve the family as a social unit?

E. Objective (multiple choice) examination questions. Choose the *best* response.

1. The historical development of group services is fixed in:
   a. the settlement movement.
   b. the youth serving organizations.
   c. the emergence of group work as a method of social work practice.
   X d. all of the above.

2. Which of the following factors contributed to the lessening of importance of the group services field of practice?
   a. growing numbers of social workers chose to enter other fields of practice, particularly those with a problem/condition orientation
   b. a change in how schools of social work were training in the group work method, leaning toward group therapy rather than traditional group service methods
   c. the development of the generalist approach to practice, abolishing group work as a distinct method of practice
   X d. all of the above

3. According to the text, for group services to be considered a valid field of practice within social welfare which of the following must happen?
   a. The profession of social work must more fully accept group work as a valid method of practice.
   b. There must be public support for the use of group service in the delivery of social welfare services.
   X c. Both of the above
   d. Group therapists must more effectively demonstrate their worth.

4. Community organization as a field of practice has as a primary focus:
   a. the services provided by individuals by the social welfare system.
   X b. larger systems, primarily communities and social welfare organizations.
   c. the services provided to various groups of people by the social welfare system.
   d. the services provided to families.

5. The historical roots of community organization practice are in:

    a. the charity/philanthropic movement.

    b. the social action activities of the settlement house movement.

    c. the formation of a professional organization of social workers specializing in community organization and the recognition of community organization as a field of practice in social work .

X d. all of the above.

6. A social worker using community organization practice methods would perform which of the following roles?

    a. community planning

    b. social program evaluation

    c. generalist role with focus on coordination of services, case management and community development

X d. all of the above

7. Social change during the current century has affected the family in which one of the following ways?

    a. caused changes in family structure

    b. contributed to the disappearance of family mutual aid.

    c. caused changes in family roles and functions

    d. contributed to a lessening of family cohesiveness and stability in some families

X e. all of the above

8. A unified national family social policy would:

    a. assist family members in coping with troubles in the family system.

X b. strengthen and preserve the family as the primary social unit.

    c. assist members of families to exhibited problems in functioning.

    d. assist only the neediest families in the U.S.

9. The national non-profit organization concerned with strengthening family life and preventing and correcting conditions that adversely affect families is:

X a. Family Service Association of America.

    b. Department of Health and Human Services.

    c. White House Conference on Families

    d. National Center on Family Policy

10. Services to families are provided by which of the following agencies?

    a. private family service agencies

b. public social service agencies
c. community mental health centers
d. religious and church affiliated agencies
X e. all of the above

Chapter 14

Old new fields of practice: industrial and rural

This chapter introduces the student to two old-new fields of social work practice — social work in the industrial setting and rural social work. Early in its history, the profession had concerns and interest in these two fields of practice; however, for many years interest declined. Recently, both of these fields have again become the concern of some social workers and there are indications that both are now developing into specific fields of practice. Industrial social work, in particular, has experienced rapid development within the last several years, providing for increased employment opportunities for social workers within business and industry. Schools of social work are developing educational programs which provide specific preparation for work within this field. In graduate and undergraduate programs located in the rural areas of the United States, the field of rural social work has remained the attention over the last twenty years. A specific body of knowledge has developed relative to this field, leading to curriculum development designed to prepare students for practice in rural settings.

A. Key points and issues

1. Industrial social work, as a field of practice, focuses on the world of work. There are many tensions within the world of work that have an impact on an individual's social functioning in the work setting. Social work intervention in the industrial setting is aimed at the interface of these tensions.

2. Social work in the industrial setting has an extensive history, dating back to the middle ages, when medieval guilds set aside funds to provide economic security in cases of accidents, old age, or death of the worker. In the United States an early concern of social work in this field was in the labor movement in the early 1900s. From 1945 through the 1960s, personnel management departments developed in many industries. These departments focused on health, education and recreational services to employees. Also during this period, programs such as workman's compensation, unemployment compensation and retirement benefits under the Social Security Act began to be

offered. From the 1970s through the present time, large industries have employed social workers in their personnel management departments to deal with the mental health problems of employees. Early programs tended to focus on problems related to alcohol and drug abuse. The number and scope of these programs have continued to grow, and most focus on expanded problem/condition areas affecting the employee. A literature base and curriculum within social work education has developed, leading to the preparation of social workers for this field of practice.

3. The industrial field of practice has developed to serve a previously unmet need. The working class population has been underserved, due to ineligibility for most public social services. The previous blocks to service provisions, the cost and stigma of programs provided in the public sector, are often overcome by providing services in the private sector.

4. Services included in industrial employees assistance programs include: counseling for personal, marital, and financial problems; crisis intervention, educational programs; health-related programs and alcohol-chemical dependency treatment; recreational services, constituents to management; and referral to community social service agencies.

5. The goals for these services rest on one of three concerns: the desire to increase financial rewards; a means to control employees and keep them productive by reducing discontent; and need to maintain profits by increasing the productivity of employees who experience problems.

6. The ways in which social workers function in the industrial setting varies from setting to setting. Three primary modes of employee assistance have developed: within the structure of industry, within the structure of the labor union, or on a contractual basis with a community social service agency.

7. There are a number of issues that must be addressed in the development of industrial-based programs. Practitioners should be aware of these issues and work toward their resolution. A primary issue exists around the goal of industrial social work. Is the goal to increase profits or production or to increase the social functioning of the employee? Is the goal to assist the industry or the union to maintain employee loyalty or to assist in insuring the primary interests and well-being of the employee? Another issue is confidentiality, insuring the employee's

right to confidentiality relative to service provision, so that information about the employee's problems does not become a means of social control by the business or industry. Another issue to be addressed: Is the work place responsible for providing services to employees who experience problems with outdated work skills or poor preparation for entering the work force? Should the overall goal of industrial social work be to maintain the status quo or to work for change so that human problems can be prevented and the work place become a more humane place? More recently the issues of retirement planning, child care, concern for older family members and the erosion of health insurance coverage for employees have come to the forefront. These issues need to be address by social workers. Like practice in other fields in which social work is not the primary profession, there is competition with other helping professions. Social work must demonstrate its expertise and how it can be of service to employer and employee.

8. In this chapter, rural social work is defined as social work practice in non-metropolitan communities (communities with a population of 50,000 or less are designated as nonmetropolitan by the U.S. Census Bureau).

9. Practice in non-metropolitan areas is different. First, the service delivery system is smaller and depends heavily on the public social service agency. The social system of a rural community functions more informally. The helping system is different, with much more reliance on self-help, natural helpers and grass-roots groups, and less reliance on formal social service delivery mechanisms. More attention is paid to ecological concerns, a key component of rural culture.

10. Rural social work has an extensive history with several forerunners in its development. In the early 1900s the Country Life Commissions emerged and had as a function the development of awareness of the needs of rural communities. The National Conference on Charities and Corrections gave some attention to the need for services to rural people during this time. During World War 1, the Home Service of the Red Cross developed a service delivery approach to rural communities. The needs of rural youth were addressed by the development of the 4-H Clubs in the 1920s. The Agricultural Extension Programs provided many programs for rural farm families. During the Depression, several of the New Deal programs were designed to assist the

rural population. The child welfare provisions of the Social Security Act of 1935 made provisions for services to children from rural areas. From the late 1960s to the present time, several events have laid the groundwork for the emergence of rural social work as a distinct field of practice. These events include: the development of new modes of social work practice that are more acceptable to rural peoples, legislation that has provided for the provision of services to rural areas, and the development of a literature base and curriculum in social work education for preparation of professionals for work in rural areas.

11. Two considerations are important when viewing social work practice in rural areas. First, the delivery system of human services is different from that of metropolitan communities. Second, there are greater differences among rural populations. Human diversity issues must be considered. Rural areas contain a very diverse population, including some minority groups that face great discrimination. Social workers must understand the diverse nature and cultures of rural peoples if they are to effectively intervene with them.

12 The informal nature of service delivery must be taken into consideration. Social workers must use the natural resource systems and adapt practice modalities to meet the needs of persons within the rural culture.

13. Social work practitioners in rural areas should be skilled in the use of crisis intervention, support, problem solving, mediating, brokering, work with multi-problem families, coordination, and program development. They need to be true generalists.

14. Many issues confront the nature of rural social work practice. Practitioners need to be aware of them. A major issue is that the rural context calls for a different kind of social work practice. Social workers must be skilled in coordinating the informal and formal systems of helping. Social workers need to see that rural communities do no always have fewer resources for helping but that they have different resources.

B. The student needs to develop the following.

1. An understanding of the definition of industrial social work and its general goals and purposes.

2. An understanding of the historical development of industrial social work, with an awareness of the factors and events which have contributed to its development.

3. An understanding of how industrial social work developed to meet the needs of an underserved population, the American worker.

4. An understanding of the tensions, issues and challenges facing the industrial social worker.

5. An understanding of the services provided by industrial employee assistance programs.

6. An understanding of the specific goals of the services provided by social workers in the industrial setting.

7. An understanding of how a social worker functions in an industrial setting and the primary modes of service delivery which are employed in these settings.

8. An awareness of and sensitivity to the issues which confront social work practice and social workers in the industrial setting. Most importantly, an awareness of how the values of industry may conflict with the values of social work practice.

9. An understanding of what constitutes rural social work and how this chapter defines it.

10 An understanding of the differentials for social work practice in non-metropolitan areas.

11. An understanding of the historical development of rural social work, its forerunners and the events which shaped its re-emergence as a distinct field of practice.

12. An understanding of the nature of social work practice in rural areas and the human diversity issues which must be considered.

13. An understanding of the informal nature of social work practice in rural areas and the need to adapt practice modalities to meet the needs of rural persons.

14 An understanding of the various roles performed by social workers in the rural setting.

15 An awareness of and sensitivity to the many issues which confront the nature of rural social work practice.

C. A variety of learning activities could be utilized in the teaching of this material. Ask practitioners from industrial settings, if available, and rural settings to speak to the class relative to their work. The instructor may also assign additional readings to the students on these fields of practice from the suggested readings list provided in the text. Conducting student discussion groups, utilizing the discussion questions in the text or in this manual may also assist the students in learning about these fields of practice. The use of case materials around practice in industrial settings or rural settings would give students some "hands on" experience in applying concepts to practice.

D. Class discussion or study questions.

1. What are the differences between industrial social work as a field of practice and other fields of practice previously studied? What **specific factors account for** the differences?

2. What events or factors account for it taking a considerable period of time for industrial social work to emerge?

3. What are the advantages and disadvantages of each of the three arrangements for the delivery of social work services in the industrial setting?

4 What has accounted for businesses and industry becoming interested in providing for mental health and other social services to their employees?

5. What are the roles that are performed by social workers in the industrial setting? Given the purposes of these roles, are there any value conflicts that might emerge for social workers in the delivery of services in the industrial setting? What issues or concerns must be resolved for effective practice to result?

6. Why has it taken so long for rural social work to be recognized as a legitimate field of social work practice?

7. What are the differences between rural populations and metropolitan populations? How do these differences affect social work practice?

8. What kinds of services are most appropriately delivered by informal helping networks and which by formal helping?

9. What are the roles performed by social workers in rural communities? What factors affect the performance of these roles? Are these roles different from those performed by social workers in different settings? Why is social work practice in rural areas truly generalist practice?

10. What issues or concerns affect the nature of social work practice in the rural setting? How can these issues and concerns best be resolved?

E. Objective (multiple choice) examination questions. Choose the *best* response.

1. Industrial social work focuses on:

   X a. the tensions within the world of work that have an impact on the employee's functioning in the work setting.
   b. the functioning of the employee in his/her family and community environment.
   c. problems and concerns of management with workers who are not productive.
   d. tensions between labor and management.

2. Which of the following was a forerunner of industrial social work?

   a. medieval guilds providing for economic security of disabled and old age employees or dependents of deceased workers
   b. the labor movement of the 1900s
   c. personal management departments which emerged in the 1960s
   X d. all of the above

3. The industrial field of practice has developed:

   a. to serve the needs of large corporations and businesses.
   X b. because the working class population has been underserved due by the social welfare systems.
   c. to increase the work output of employees.
   d. because the social welfare system cannot meet the needs of this population.

4. The primary goal of the services provided by the industrial social worker is:

   X a. to provide services to employees who experience problems so that they become more productive employees leading to increased profits for the industry.
   b. to increase financial rewards.
   c. to control employees by reducing discontent.
   d. to reduce employee turnover rates.

5. The mode of service delivery in industrial settings in which a community social service agency contracts with the firm to provide services to employees is:

   a. employee assistance program.
   b. labor union assistance program.
   X c. purchase of service contract arrangement.
   d. Community contact assistance program.

6. The primary issue which produces value conflicts for social workers in the industrial setting is:

   a. confidentiality.

    b. assisting the industry in maintaining employee loyalty.

X c. increasing profits or production versus increasing the employees social functioning.

    d. control versus social benefit perspective.

7. In this chapter, rural social work is defined as social work practice in:

    a. communities of 2,500 or less.

    b. communities of 3,000 or less.

    c. communities of 5,000 or less.

X d. communities of 50,000 or less (non-metropolitan areas).

8. Which of the following is not a differential for practice in a non-metropolitan area?

    a. service delivery system is smaller—dependence on public social services

    b. social system of rural communities more informal

    c. there is more reliance on formal services mechanisms.

X d. There is more reliance on natural helping and self-help resources.

9. Rural social work emerged in the late 1960s as a result of:

    a. new modes of social work practice that are more acceptable to rural peoples.

    b. legislative action providing increased funding for service delivery in rural areas.

    c. the development of a literature base, and curriculum development in social work education for preparation of professions for work in rural areas.

X d. all of the above.

10. The overall mode of social work practice which has been found the most effective in rural communities is:

    a. therapist mode of practice

    b. community developer.

X c. the generalist.

    d. group worker.

Part III

The Contemporary Social Welfare System

This part of the text serves as a summary for the book. Chapter 15 presents an analytic framework by which students can evaluate the various components of the social welfare system. This framework also provides the students with a means of identifying the linkages between the various components of the system .

Chapter 15

The contemporary social welfare system

Whereas the previous chapters of the text broke the social welfare system down into its component parts, this chapter serves as a summary for the entire text, this chapter discusses the system as a whole, and provides a framework by which students can analyze the relationships and themes presented in the text. This is done to assist the student in gaining an integrated picture of the U.S. social welfare system. The framework will assist the student in understanding how any response to human needs made by the social welfare system can be analyzed and evaluated.

The chapter also discusses major issues which confront the contemporary social welfare system. While no attempt has been made to provide solutions to those issues, several changes which have been suggested will be discussed. Several contemporary social problems with a focus on the capacity of the social welfare system to respond to them are presented, and the future of the social work profession as a part of the social welfare system is also considered. Last, suggestions are made relative to what further steps the student can take to gain a greater understanding of the system.

A. Because this chapter serves as a summary for the entire text, and reviews much material that was previously discussed, this concluding chapter of the instructor's manual will follow a different format than used in the previous chapters. The authors believe that the best use of this material is in the development of learning activities which utilize the framework for analysis of the social welfare system provided in the chapter. Class discussion or study questions are provided and focus on the major issues identified in the chapter.

B. The development of learning activities is essential to the teaching of this material. The instructor may want to use the suggested activities offered here or create other activities that would assist student learning of this material. For instance, there may be problem/conditions, specific population groups or other social welfare issues that are of concern in your region of the country, locale or state, which you may wish students to address using the materials in this chapter. Whatever activities are used, instructors should keep in mind the central theme presented throughout the text, *Human Need,* and focus on the major impetus for the development of the social welfare system as a means for assisting individuals, families, groups and communities in meeting their needs.

C. Suggested learning activities

1. To assist students in learning how to use the analytic framework provided in this chapter, divide the class into groups and have them review the framework and the example of its use in the text. Assign each group a different human-problem topic (such as the frail elderly or homeless, violence, aids, health care, feminization of poverty, abortion, unemployment, or housing problems) and have them evaluate the responses that have been made or could be made by the social welfare system to their human-problem topic using the framework for analysis. This learning activity will require them to identify the following:

   a. the conditions which gave rise to the needs and problems;

   b. the needs present in the past or contemporary situation;

   c. the social welfare arrangements that have or could be used to respond to the needs identified and the factors which have influenced the development of the arrangements;

   d. the fields of practice that would be appropriate given the problem-need situation;

   e. how social workers working in the fields of practice identified have or might intervene to deal with the problems or needs in the situation.

2. Divide the class into groups and assign one or more of the following class study or discussion questions. Have each group make an oral report to the class, summarizing their discussion of these questions.

D. Class discussion or study questions

   1. Have particular arrangements to meet human needs developed more from tradition than from a careful analysis of the ability of the arrangement to best meet the needs of people?

   2. Has the fields of practice structure as the organizing mechanism for service delivery allowed the system to develop in a piecemeal manner, compartmentalizing problems so that a holistic view of the individual, family and community are overlooked?

3. Does the current structure prevent the various parts of the system from working together to meet the needs of individuals and families? Are the current fields of practice the most appropriate ones for the contemporary scene or merely relics of historical development? Are there new fields of practice that should be developed?

4. How can consideration be given to how best to provide a structure of social welfare that has equality across the United States, yet provides for appropriate measures of local control?

5. Are the health care, mental health, education, and corrections systems really a part of the overall social welfare system? If so, what reasons can be given as to why they should be considered as such? How has the profession of social work served as a link between these systems and the overall social welfare system?

6. What roles and functions should the BSW and MSW assume within the social welfare system? Which tasks can each best perform? Other professionals (e.g., nurses, psychologists) work within the system. What roles and functions should they perform? What should be the relationship of the social worker to these professionals?

7. Should all social welfare services be delivered by professionals? Should paraprofessionals, volunteers, natural helpers and self-help groups be involved in the delivery of services? What should be the relationship of professionals to these groups?

8. How should the social welfare system function to provide for the needs of persons who are affected by poverty, racism, and discrimination? What can the system do to eliminate these conditions that prevent individuals and families from meeting their own needs?

9. Concerning resource availability, what resources should governmental bodies provide to people? Which governmental unit—federal state or local—should provide such resources? What resources can informal helping systems in the community provide? How should government support these natural helping systems?

10. Given the current economic and political situation, expansion in social welfare programs is not likely to occur. How can needed services and resources be provided to people with little or no increased funding?

11. Is the provision of social welfare, through its various arrangements and fields of practice, carried out from the residual or universal approach? Support your answer by giving reasons for your choice. In your view, which of these two approaches should the system be structured so as to provide? Again, support your answer.

12. Assess one of the proposals for reorganizing the social welfare system presented in the chapter (e.g., the Carter plan, Withorn's strategies, or Stoesz's ,,Corporate welfare,,). What are its strengths, its limitations? What influences would need to be made for the adoption of the proposal? What factors might influence the rejection of the proposal?

13. Does the nature of social work practice need to change in response to recent political and social changes that have cutback services and curtailed resources? Should social workers be more politically active? What contributions have been made by professional social work organizations in bringing about political change that benefits the poor or other disenfranchised groups?

NOTES

NOTES